100
THINGS TO KNOW ABOUT
THE
OCEANS

Usborne Quicklinks

For links to websites and videos where you can find out more about many of the facts in this book, watch amazing ocean wildlife and discover other secrets of the seas, go to **usborne.com/Quicklinks** and enter the keywords: **things to know about the oceans**.

Here are some of the things you can do at the websites we recommend:

• Meet the small – but deadly – blue-ringed octopus
• Take a virtual tour of an underwater science lab
• See how sperm whales, parrotfish and other sea creatures sleep
• Dive into a frozen world beneath the Antarctic ice
• See inside a Dutch windmill that helped turn the ocean into farmland
• Find out about the Great Pacific Garbage Patch and how to prevent plastic pollution

100
THINGS TO
KNOW ABOUT
THE
OCEANS

Written by
Jerome Martin, Alex Frith, Alice James,
Lan Cook, Minna Lacey and Lizzie Cope

Illustrated by
Dominique Byron, Dale Edwin Murray,
Federico Mariani, Shaw Nielsen and Jake Williams

Designed by
Jenny Offley, Winsome D'Abreu, Tilly Kitching,
Lenka Hrehova and Samuel Gorham

1 Planet Earth...

should be called Planet Ocean.

The name for our planet, in almost every language, is also a word that means *ground* or *soil* or just plain *dirt*. But, if alien explorers visited our planet, it's the *water* on its surface that they'd find most remarkable...

Ooh, look at that planet! It's covered in water.

What shall we name it?

First planet we've seen for light-years that has liquid water on the surface.

Bluetopia!

Oceanus!

Waterworld!

WATERY PLANET KEY FACTS

Planet's surface is mostly water.
Surface area: **71% water** and **29% land**

Most of planet's water is salty.
97% of it is found in seas and oceans.

Planet's life is mostly under water.
50–80% of planet's creatures live in oceans.

2 Icebergs fizz...
thanks to ancient bubbles.

Most icebergs are made of ice, built up layer by layer, over time. Each layer contains tiny air bubbles that were trapped as the water around them froze. When icebergs melt in the ocean, those bubbles burst and air whooshes to the surface.

FIZZZZZ

You gotta listen to this.

Hydrophone

DRIP

POP

WHOOSH

CSHHH

To find out what a hydrophone is, and for definitions of other unfamiliar words, turn to the glossary on pages 124-125.

The fizzing and popping is the sound of *centuries* worth of air being released from tiny bubbles along the iceberg's sides.

3 The biggest crowds on Earth...
are fish.

The largest recorded gathering of any animal was Atlantic herring. Fishermen have always known that herring can sometimes form *enormous* groups called **shoals** – but it's only since the early 2000s that scientists have started to record the numbers.

Herring typically swim in deep waters, but move to shallow seas in shoals that can last for many hours.

These herring are packed so tightly that we can't sail through them. We're stuck!

I've heard that a single shoal can contain **250 MILLION FISH** and weigh over **50,000 TONS**.

And they can cover an area **40km (25 miles) wide**. We're going to be here for a while!

Scientists don't know exactly *why* herring form these mega-shoals, but most believe it helps them to find mates.

4 Mountains under the sea...

have lush peaks and bare bottoms.

Mighty underwater mountains, known as **seamounts**, rise up from parts of the seabed. The peaks of these seamounts are often teeming with life, while their bases are barren and rocky – the opposite of mountains on land.

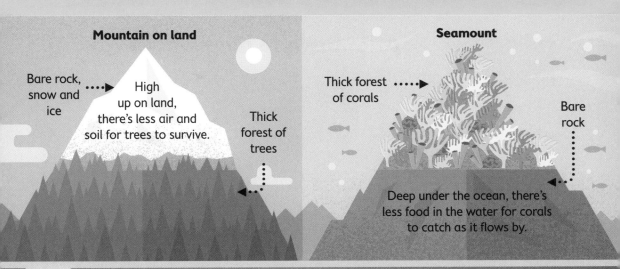

Mountain on land

Bare rock, snow and ice ·····➤

High up on land, there's less air and soil for trees to survive.

Thick forest of trees

Seamount

Thick forest ····➤ of corals

Bare rock

Deep under the ocean, there's less food in the water for corals to catch as it flows by.

5 Lights-out for pirates...

was at 8 o'clock.

Pirates are often considered wild and lawless, but many pirate captains enforced strict rules to ensure a safer life at sea. These included putting out candles and lanterns at a set time.

In the 18th century, Welsh pirate Black Bart Roberts wrote a list of rules for his crew to follow. He insisted all lights went out at 8pm to prevent fire – a particularly dangerous hazard on a wooden ship.

6 Heading north to go east...

is the secret to crossing the Atlantic.

The waters of the northern Atlantic move in a steady swirl known as the **Atlantic Gyre**. For hundreds of years, sailors voyaging from west to east learned that the fastest route was to steer north into the gyre – even though that meant starting off in the wrong direction.

Atlantic Gyre map

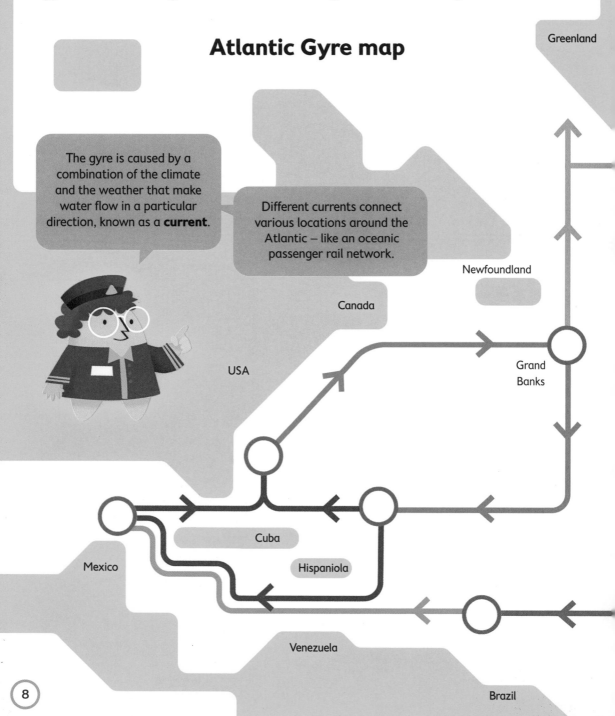

The gyre is caused by a combination of the climate and the weather that make water flow in a particular direction, known as a **current**.

Different currents connect various locations around the Atlantic – like an oceanic passenger rail network.

Greenland

Newfoundland

Canada

USA

Grand Banks

Cuba

Mexico

Hispaniola

Venezuela

Brazil

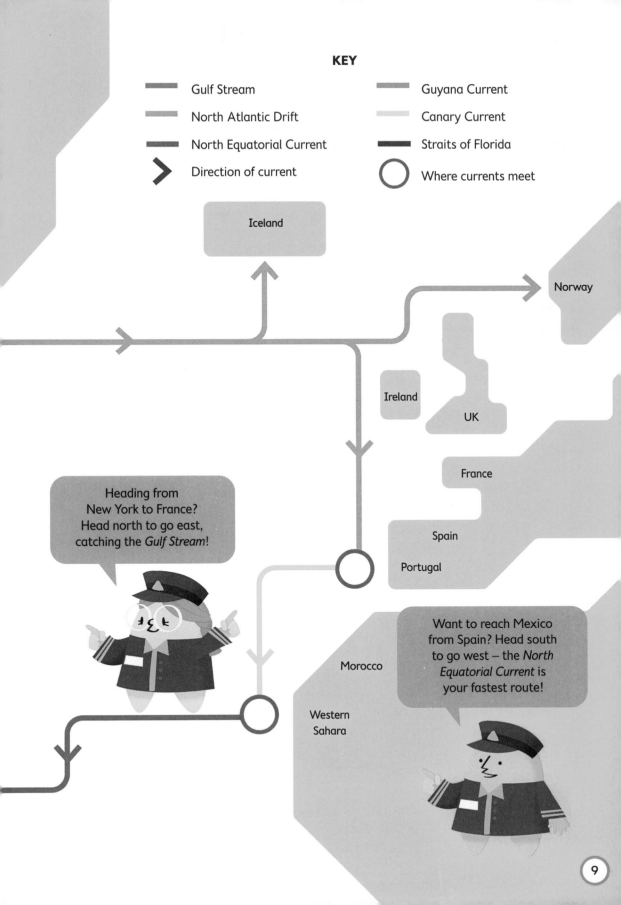

7 Black sand beaches...

form in the blink of an eye.

The most common type of beach sand is made from pale quartz crystals worn down into tiny grains by wind and waves over thousands of years. But one kind of sand can form almost instantly, with entire beaches appearing overnight.

Overnight beaches can appear when lava (molten rock from a volcanic eruption) pours into the sea. Think of it as a recipe with just two ingredients...

Contains: ICE COLD
SEAWATER

USBORNE BEACH-AT-HOME INSTANT RANGE

FOR LUSH
BLACK SAND
JUST ADD
LAVA

BLACK VOLCANIC SAND INSTANT FORMULA

Original Hawaiian recipe! As seen in Punalu'u Beach, Waipi'o Beach, Kaimu Bay and MANY MORE

*Lava must be piping hot. Please use proper safety equipment, as molten rock will instantly shatter and explode on contact with cold water, producing lustrous black volcanic sand.

8 Way, hey, haul away Joe...

helped raise up the sails that made sailing ships go.

Work songs called **sea shanties** were an essential part of a sailor's life.

When a sailor signed up for a voyage afloat,

With a way, hey, haul away Joe!

The skipper would ask, "Lad, can you hold a note?"

And you haul away hard or it's under you go!

"Can you warble or trill, can you singsong or croon?"

With a way, hey, haul away Joe!

"For we can't sail the ship if you can't hold a tune."

With the wild wind above and the water below!

Yes, for many long years aboard tall sailing ships,

With a way, hey, haul away Joe!

Men pulled every rope with a song on their lips.

And you haul away hard or it's under you go!

The rhythmical songs helped the crews work in time,

With a way, hey, haul away Joe!

They tugged on the beat and they heaved on the rhyme —

With the wild wind above and the water below!

9 Sperm whales stand up...

to go to sleep.

When sperm whales need a nap, they do what scientists call a **drift-dive**. They take up a straight, vertical position, drifting just beneath the surface of the water.

Shhh!

A few times per day, sperm whales fall into a deep, motionless sleep for 10-15 minutes at a time.

Sperm whales usually form groups of five or six to sleep.

They spend just 7% of their lives resting – getting less sleep than ANY other mammal in the world.

Whales don't breathe while they sleep – they need to be conscious to take a breath.

10 An upside-down flag...

means trouble afloat.

When a ship at sea is in distress, the crew can send out a call for help using radios, phones or satellite beacons. But if all else fails, all you need... is a flag.

These are distress signals recognized by sailors around the world. Some have been in use for centuries.

National flag upside down

National flag knotted in the middle

····N
····C

"N" and "C" flags, from a set of alphabetical signal flags used at sea

Crew member waving arms up and down

Square black flag over a black ball

Red star flares or rockets

Oh, NOW she tells us!

Couldn't you have mentioned this BEFORE our ship sank?!

Captains are required by international laws and conventions to come to the aid of another vessel in distress.

11 New looks and fresh styles...

keep cuttlefish safe at sea.

Cuttlefish have an amazing ability to change the shade, pattern and even texture of their bodies to match their surroundings. Scientists call this **adaptive camouflage**.

CUTTLEFISH FASHION SHOW
A DISGUISE FOR EVERY OCCASION

Cuttlefish are a type of soft-bodied sea creature related to squids and octopuses. They often live in reefs.

Pink and orange shades keep a cuttlefish hidden in bright, healthy coral.

As a cuttlefish moves, its pattern changes to blend in with its background and lets it go unnoticed by predators and prey.

Pale camouflage blends in with the white, bleached coral that fills a lot of reefs.

Adding rocks and stones on its back makes a cuttlefish's disguise even better.

Cuttlefish can break up their outline using rocks and pebbles. This is called **disruptive camouflage**.

Cuttlefish change pattern using specialized cells called **chromatophores**. Chromatophores are little sacs full of pigment that the cuttlefish can expand or shrink to change shade.

Black camouflage is perfect for disguise at night or in dark corners.

Your turn to show us your new look!

To blend in with fronds and seaweed, cuttlefish take on greens and a leafy texture.

The cuttlefishes' ability to change pattern is particularly baffling to scientists because cuttlefish can't see different shades — their eyes only work in black and white.

Not all pattern changes are designed for camouflage. Cuttlefish also adapt their looks to help them communicate with each other.

Cuttlefish adopt this striped outfit when they are in fighting mode.

15

Biggest, fastest, longest...

oldest, loudest, deepest.

Biggest...
eyeball
27cm (11in) across

The colossal squid has the biggest eye
in the animal kingdom. Each one is
roughly the size of a bowling ball.

Fastest...
punch
23m (75ft) per second

The mantis shrimp strikes its prey with the fastest and
most powerful punch of any animal. If humans could
throw a punch at just a tenth of the mantis shrimp's
speed, we'd be able to throw a baseball into orbit.

Longest...
teeth
Just over 1cm (0.4in)

It may sound small, but Sloane's viperfish
has the longest teeth of any animal relative to
the size of its head. Just imagine your teeth
being half the size of your head.

Oldest...
living animal
11,000 years (approximately)

Monorhaphis chuni is a deep-sea glass sponge found in the China Sea and the Indian Ocean. It is the oldest living creature discovered so far. Humans were still in the Stone Age at the start of its life.

Loudest...
voice
236 decibels

Sperm whales are the loudest animals on the planet. Human speech typically reaches around 60 decibels. The creaks and clicks sperm whales make are almost as loud as an atomic bomb exploding.

Deepest...
fish
8,178m (26,830ft)

The Mariana snailfish is the ocean's deepest swimming fish. It is one of the few creatures that can withstand the crushing water pressure at the Mariana Trench, the oceans' deepest point – roughly equivalent to 1,600 elephants standing on its head.

13 The Red Sea isn't red...

but the Yellow Sea is yellow.

There are several seas around the world whose names *suggest* waters of a particular and startling shade: bright Red, dazzling White, inky Black – but in reality, the Yellow Sea is the only one that lives up to its name.

Yellow Sea

Location: South China Sea, between China and Korea

Reason for its name:
Sand from the Gobi Desert gives its water a yellow tinge.

Red Sea

Location: between Egypt and Arabia

Possible reason for its name:
Large patches of red bacteria occasionally multiply on its surface, making it slightly pink or red in places.

White Sea

Location: northern Russia

Possible reasons for its name:
a) It is covered in ice for up to six months each year.
b) Its clear surface often reflects the clouds in the sky, making the water appear white.

Black Sea

Location: between Russia, Ukraine and Turkey

Possible reasons for its name:
a) Black sludge on the sea floor is sometimes churned up by storms, darkening the water.
b) It is home to very few living things.

14 One tiny sea creature...

keeps us breathing.

Most of the oxygen we breathe is made in the ocean by plants and other living things. But around a fifth of that oxygen is produced by just *one* species of a plant-like bacteria – a phytoplankton called **prochlorococcus**.

It's tiny...
It would take 100, laid end to end, to equal the width of a single human hair.

...but there's a lot of it.
Prochlorococcus is one the most numerous life forms on Earth. It's estimated there are up to **3 octillion** worldwide – that's 3 followed by 27 zeros!

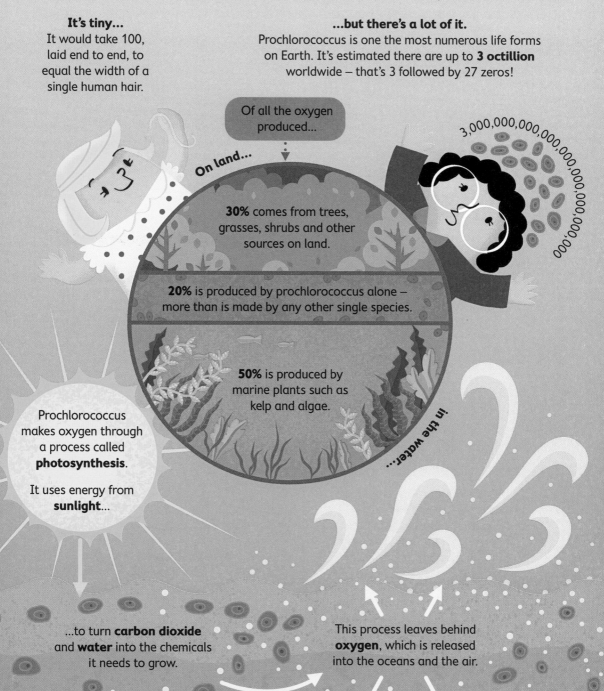

3,000,000,000,000,000,000,000,000,000

Of all the oxygen produced...

On land...

30% comes from trees, grasses, shrubs and other sources on land.

20% is produced by prochlorococcus alone – more than is made by any other single species.

50% is produced by marine plants such as kelp and algae.

...in the water...

Prochlorococcus makes oxygen through a process called **photosynthesis**.

It uses energy from **sunlight**...

...to turn **carbon dioxide** and **water** into the chemicals it needs to grow.

This process leaves behind **oxygen**, which is released into the oceans and the air.

15 The Great Tea Race of 1866...

was won – and lost – by the same two ships.

From the 1840s, speedy sailing ships called **tea clippers** carried tea from China to the UK. The first harvest of each season was the most valuable, and the ships raced each other to bring it to London. The winner got the best price for the tea and a cash prize – until it all went wrong in 1866...

On the 28th of May, five clippers left the Chinese port of Fuzhou, just hours apart.

The ships sped toward London, each loaded with enough tea to brew about **240 million cups**.

Ariel ....

Taeping .....

16 The ship of the future...

could look a lot like the ships of the past.

In the 1870s, new ships were built with steam engines and propellers. The age of sail seemed to be over. But while engine-powered ships have ruled the seas for over 100 years, engineers are constantly working to improve on ship designs – and some of these even include sails...

1840s-1880s: Tea clipper
• Narrow hull and sharp bow designed to cut through waves
• Row of three towering masts
• Can carry more than 30 sails

TOO SLOW

1870s-1940s: Steam freighter
• Narrow steel hull and blunt bow
• Screw propeller powered by steam engine

TOO SMALL

Newspapers everywhere reported on their progress as they sailed non-stop for 99 days. It was one of the greatest races in sailing history.

At last, two of the five reached London within minutes of each other. The victorious rivals agreed to share the prize...

...BUT: seven days *after* the Great Tea Race began, a ship called SS *Erl King* left Fuzhou, also loaded with tea.

It had a steam-driven propeller to assist its sails, and arrived in London 15 days *ahead* of the clippers. Its tea sold for the highest price.

The tea clippers' prize was never given again — and soon, steam engines replaced sails entirely.

TOO DIRTY

1940s-Today: Bulk cargo carrier
• Wide steel hull and rounded bow
• Row of cranes for loading and unloading cargo, such as grain or coal
• Powerful engine uses cheap diesel fuel that pollutes the sea and the air

The main search is for a cleaner fuel, but some engineers are testing new ships that *combine* sails and engines to cut down on fuel use.

Coming soon: Sail freighter
• Narrower hull and sharper bow
• Row of rigid sails shaped like plane wings and managed by computers
• Slower, smaller, but much cleaner

17 Acid rain and salty rocks...

make seawater salty.

When the world's oceans formed over 3.8 billion years ago, they were full of fresh water. And they would have stayed that way, if not for rain...

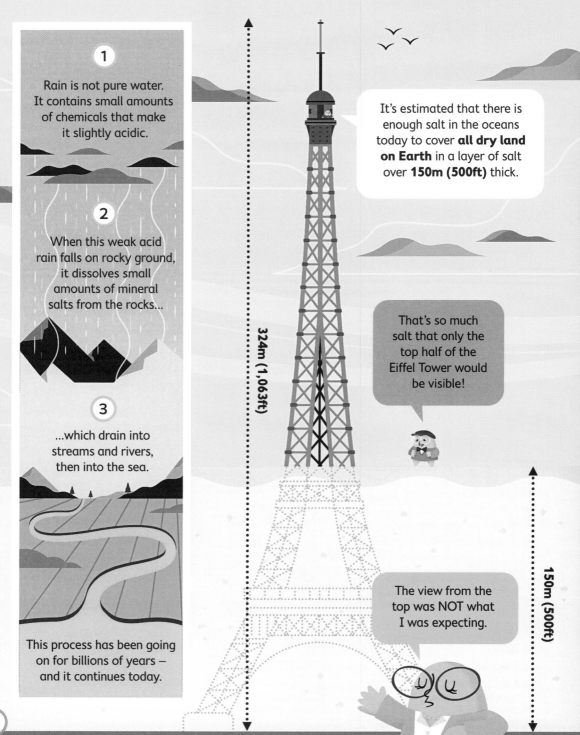

1
Rain is not pure water. It contains small amounts of chemicals that make it slightly acidic.

2
When this weak acid rain falls on rocky ground, it dissolves small amounts of mineral salts from the rocks...

3
...which drain into streams and rivers, then into the sea.

This process has been going on for billions of years — and it continues today.

It's estimated that there is enough salt in the oceans today to cover **all dry land on Earth** in a layer of salt over **150m (500ft)** thick.

That's so much salt that only the top half of the Eiffel Tower would be visible!

The view from the top was NOT what I was expecting.

324m (1,063ft)

150m (500ft)

18 A woman aboard was bad luck...

unless she was about to give birth.

Traditionally, European seafarers were a superstitious – but inconsistent – bunch. It was once seen as a sign of good fortune if a baby was born on a voyage – but bad luck to have a woman on board at all.

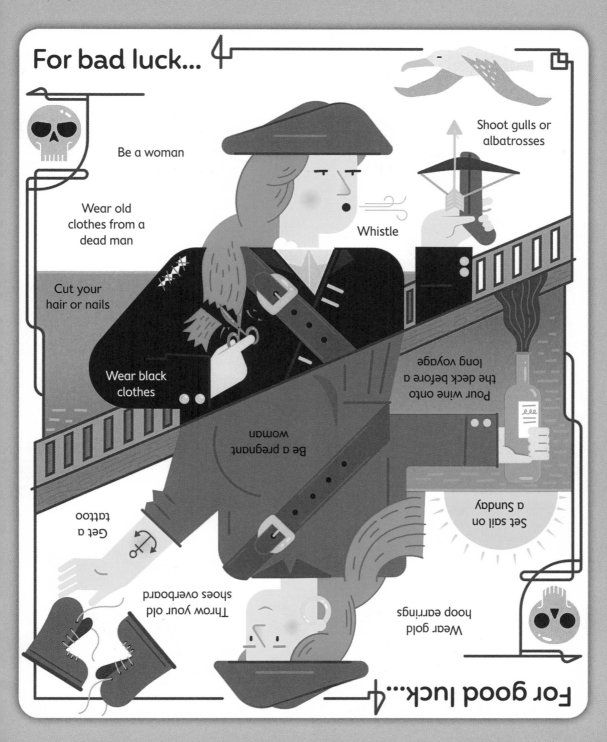

For bad luck...

Be a woman

Wear old clothes from a dead man

Cut your hair or nails

Wear black clothes

Whistle

Shoot gulls or albatrosses

Pour wine onto the deck before a long voyage

Be a pregnant woman

Get a tattoo

Throw your old shoes overboard

Wear gold hoop earrings

Set sail on a Sunday

For good luck...

19 There's a Garbage Patch...

at the end of every Pacific current.

Water continually moves through oceans in fast-moving, long-distance channels called **currents**. Follow these pieces of plastic waste dropped into the North Pacific Ocean to see their final destinations, where the currents take them...

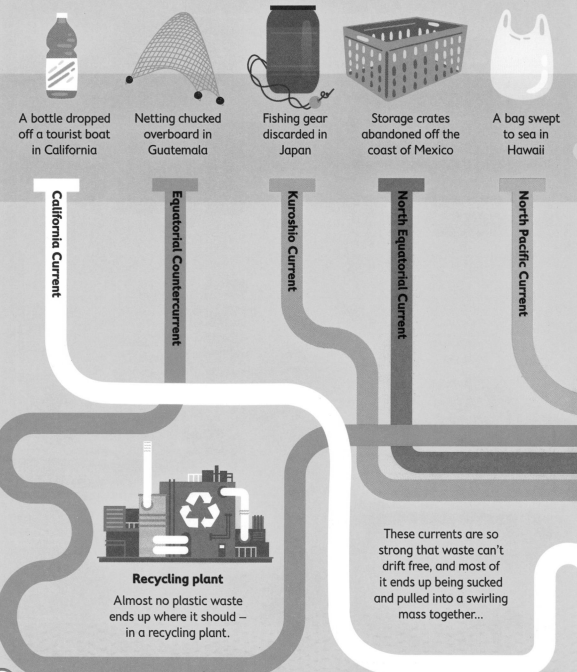

A bottle dropped off a tourist boat in California

Netting chucked overboard in Guatemala

Fishing gear discarded in Japan

Storage crates abandoned off the coast of Mexico

A bag swept to sea in Hawaii

California Current

Equatorial Countercurrent

Kuroshio Current

North Equatorial Current

North Pacific Current

Recycling plant

Almost no plastic waste ends up where it should — in a recycling plant.

These currents are so strong that waste can't drift free, and most of it ends up being sucked and pulled into a swirling mass together...

Landfill site

Hardly any waste ends up in a landfill site.

Washed ashore

Some waste gets washed onto beaches.

The Great Pacific Garbage Patch

Almost ALL waste ends up in **The Great Pacific Garbage Patch**.
It is a colossal stretch of floating waste, more than **three times** the size of France.
There are four other patches like this in oceans around the world.

20 When hermit crabs move home...

they bring their own security guards.

Hermit crabs live inside discarded snail shells. For extra protection, one type of hermit crab places one or more sea anemones on its shell to act as security guards. And from then on, they stick together no matter what.

When a hermit crab outgrows its shell...

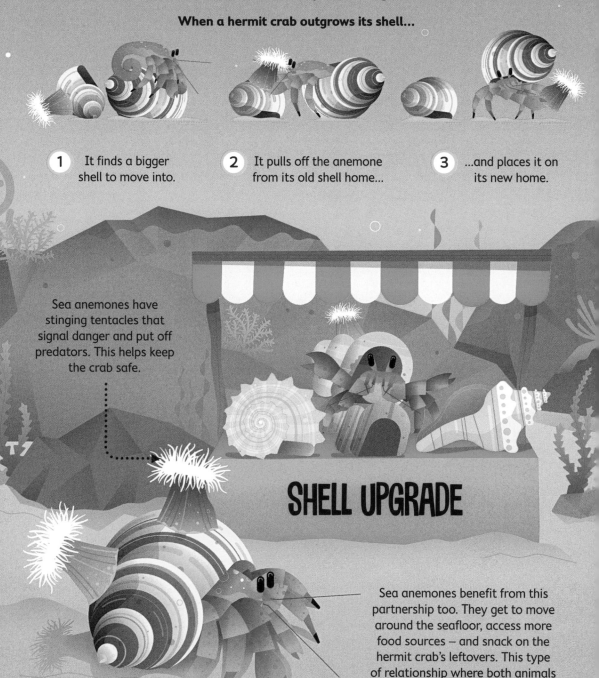

1 It finds a bigger shell to move into.

2 It pulls off the anemone from its old shell home...

3 ...and places it on its new home.

Sea anemones have stinging tentacles that signal danger and put off predators. This helps keep the crab safe.

SHELL UPGRADE

Sea anemones benefit from this partnership too. They get to move around the seafloor, access more food sources — and snack on the hermit crab's leftovers. This type of relationship where both animals benefit is known as **symbiosis**.

21 Shaking creatures...

make shorelines glow.

Some bays and shorelines around the world are filled with tiny aquatic creatures called **dinoflagellates**. These dinoflagellates make some seas glow in the dark.

Dinoflagellates are single-celled organisms that live in the sea. Many of them are **bioluminescent** – meaning they can make their own light.

A chemical called **luciferin** inside the dinoflagellates' bodies makes a short, bright flash of light.

In most species, making light is triggered when the creatures are shaken. That means the light is brightest where waves hit the shore, or where people disturb the water...

Scientists aren't completely sure why this happens, but it might be to help scare off predators.

22 If the Arctic Ocean filled a cup...

the Pacific Ocean would fill a bucket.

The Pacific Ocean is so wide and so deep, it holds roughly HALF of all the world's seawater. The smallest ocean is the Arctic, which holds just a small fraction of that.

EARTH

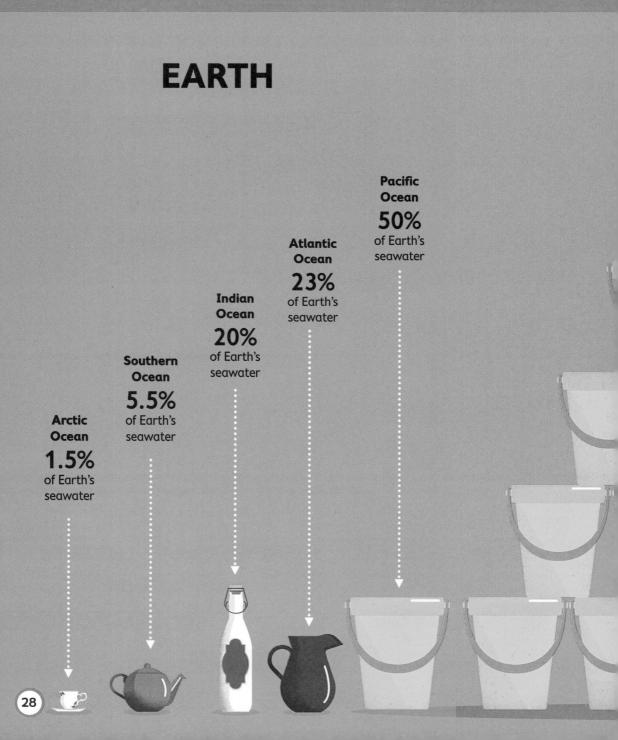

Pacific Ocean
50%
of Earth's seawater

Atlantic Ocean
23%
of Earth's seawater

Indian Ocean
20%
of Earth's seawater

Southern Ocean
5.5%
of Earth's seawater

Arctic Ocean
1.5%
of Earth's seawater

23 Fifty-three Pacific Oceans...

are hidden beneath the surface of Ganymede.

Earth isn't actually the wettest known world. Ganymede, Jupiter's largest moon, is far smaller than Earth. But beneath its surface of rock and ice, scientists have detected signs of a mind-bogglingly vast saltwater ocean.

GANYMEDE

Scientists aren't sure just *how* big Ganymede's buried ocean is, but the best estimate is that it contains about

53 TIMES

as much water as Earth's biggest ocean.

Estimated total volume of Ganymede's ocean:

34.5 billion km^3

(8.5 billion cubic miles)

That's many more Pacifics than can fit on this page...

24 A drop of hagfish slime...

can stop a shark attack.

Hagfish are boneless, sightless, eel-shaped fish that feed mainly on dead creatures at the bottom of the sea. Over time, they have developed an excellent – if slightly gross – way to defend against predators: slime.

When attacked by predators such as larger fish or sharks, a hagfish releases goo from pores along the length of its body.

Under water, the goo expands quickly to **10,000 times** its original volume...

...creating a sticky, smothering cloud of slime that clogs the attacker's mouth, eyes and gills.

To clean the slime off *itself*, a hagfish simply ties its boneless body into a knot. Then, it slides the knot from one end of itself to the other, squeezing away the slime.

25 One person's pirate...

was another's hero.

The simplest definition of a pirate is a seaborne criminal. But real, historical pirates often looked just like other seafarers – people who might even be heroes, depending on your point of view...

Know your PIRATES

The essential guide for 17th-century sailors

Life at sea can be confusing. Just remember: the main difference between a pirate, a privateer and a corsair is whether or not **YOU** are their preferred prey.

Tell at a glance who's fair and who's foul.

The wicked PIRATE

Preferred prey:
YOU – and anyone else with a ship worth looting

Habitat:
Anywhere at sea

Season:
All year

Flag:
Black

These are seafarers who will attack and loot anyone. They are considered criminals the world over.

The heroic PRIVATEER

Preferred prey:
YOUR ENEMIES

Habitat:
Atlantic Ocean and Caribbean Sea

Season:
Wartime only

Flag:
Your country

These are pirates licensed by **YOUR** King or Queen to attack and loot ships belonging to enemy countries.

The vicious CORSAIR

Preferred prey:
Anyone at war with his government – including **YOU**

Habitat:
Atlantic Ocean and Caribbean Sea

Season:
Wartime only

Flag:
An enemy country

These pirates, also known as Freebooters or Buccaneers, are licensed by a country's government to pursue its enemies.

26 Good manners...

make good surfers.

The best surf spots can get very crowded. So surfers around the world rely on their own etiquette – a system of informal rules that help ensure everyone behaves politely, stays safe and gets their fair share of waves.

Surfers gather in a zone called the **line-up** – just beyond the point where waves start to break. Here, they wait their turn to catch a wave.

Rule 1: Don't snake
Snaking is when you paddle around someone to catch a wave before it's your turn.

Rule 2: Don't drop in
This is when you try to ride a wave but another surfer has priority.

This surfer is closest to the peak of the wave – the point where it begins to break. She has **priority**. No one else is allowed to ride her wave.

This surfer is dropping in.

Rule 3: Don't paddle out through the zone where people are surfing
To avoid possible collisions, paddle around this zone to get to the line-up.

Rule 4: Hold on to your board
A loose surfboard can tumble through the water and injure someone.

Rule 5: Respect the locals
Every surf spot has its own traditions and customs. Visitors should take the time to talk to and learn from the locals.

Hi, I'm new here. How are the waves today?

Over time, surfers have developed their own slang.

Dude, that last set was totally gnarly. I went over the falls on a macking double overhead.*

Did you see that goofy-footed grom hanging ten on a malibu? She's awesome.†

* The last group of waves was very large and violent. I fell all the way down the face of a powerful wave twice my height.

† Did you see that kid, who generally surfs with her right foot forward, riding a wave while standing on the very tip of her long surfboard? She's awesome.

but they're listening.

Inside their shells, oysters have tiny hairs that can sense vibrations caused by sound. But, nowadays, the natural sounds of the ocean – waves, singing whales, snapping shrimp – are being drowned out by human-made noise.

The sound of a cargo ship's engine and propeller is deafening, and it can carry for dozens of miles underwater. The noise can harm all kinds of sea life – from whales to oysters. Oysters usually keep their shells slightly open, so they can breathe and feed – but when they hear the intense racket of a cargo ship, they clamp their shells tightly shut.

This is bad for the oysters – and for the oceans in which they live. Oysters filter the water all around them, sifting out food and other particles. A healthy bed of oysters can help keep the ocean clean.

Luckily, there is a way to reduce the noise pollution from cargo ships: simply by getting them to slow down.

Shipwrecks, bombs, volcanoes...
Alvin has faced them all.

Piloted by a crew of two, *Alvin* is a submersible that explores the oceans up to 4,500m (14,800ft) below the surface. *Alvin* has been on many adventures since it was built in 1965 – and is still exploring today.

1966
Alvin helped find an unexploded hydrogen bomb that had fallen into the ocean near Spain.

1968
A cable lowering *Alvin* into the sea snapped, sending it down and down.

The crew escaped...

1984
Alvin found living things in cold, sunless water at the bottom of the Gulf of Mexico.

1979
In the Pacific Ocean, *Alvin* discovered "black smokers" – deep-sea volcanoes or hydrothermal vents.

...and 10 months later *Alvin* was recovered from the Atlantic seabed.

1986
Using robot camera *Jason Jr,* *Alvin* took the first detailed photos of the wreck of the *Titanic* in the north Atlantic.

2018
After several upgrades, *Alvin* completed its 5,000th dive, in the Gulf of California.

29 The very biggest ships...

could carry *900 MILLION* copies of this book.

Nine out of ten things in the world are transported by ship – usually in big, steel boxes called **containers**.

A standard container is 6.1m (20ft) long, 2.44m (8ft) wide and 2.59m (8ft, 6in) high.

At any one time, up to **6 million containers** are being transported across the oceans.

30 The top of Everest...

was once at the bottom of the ocean.

The world's highest mountain peak is made from a type of rock called marine limestone. It's called that because it was once part of an ancient seabed.

500 million years ago, in a warm, shallow sea, a tiny creature dares to dream...

Someday, I'll soar among the clouds.

Ha, ha, ha!

Dream on!

Moments later, a landslide covers the seabed – and the prehistoric animals!

Oh, crumbs.

Aw, man!

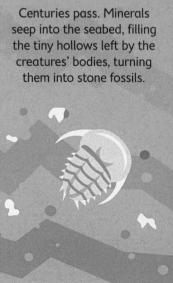

Centuries pass. Minerals seep into the seabed, filling the tiny hollows left by the creatures' bodies, turning them into stone fossils.

Some of the very largest container ships can carry as many as **21,000 containers**.

A ship that size could carry about **42,000** cars, or **500,000** fridge-freezers, or **174,300,000** boxes of breakfast cereal.

The seabed lies at the point where two land masses meet. They constantly push and grind against each other.

RUMBLE

RUMBLE

Over millions of years, the slow collision of these land masses pushes the seabed inch by inch up into the air — creating a new mountain range, now known as the Himalayas.

Height above sea level: 5km (3.1 miles) — and rising.

Mount Everest today: some dreams *do* come true.

Height above sea level: nearly 9km (5.6 miles) — and *still* rising.

The Land God Made in Anger...

is littered with bleached bones and broken ships.

One of the world's deadliest stretches of ocean runs along the coast of Namibia, in Africa. It's known in English as the *Skeleton Coast*, taking its name from the wrecks and bones that litter the sands. Its original name, in a local language, is the *Land God Made in Anger*.

Cold, unpredictable **currents** along the coast baffle navigators...

...and create dense blankets of **fog** that hide the looming dangers of the shore.

Strong **winds** blow toward the coast, pushing ships toward sandbanks and shallow waters...

...and the heavy **surf** crashes so constantly and violently that no lifeboat or raft can ever be launched from the beach.

More than **1,000 shipwrecks** clutter the sands of the Skeleton Coast, along with the bones of countless sea creatures... and sailors.

Beyond the beach lies barren **desert** and **marshland**... and little hope of rescue.

32 Here be monsters...

and chickens!?

For many centuries, mapmakers filled their maps with decorative images, some of which also represented things like safety, danger or unknown creatures. Over time, as people learned more about the seas, the images and their meanings changed...

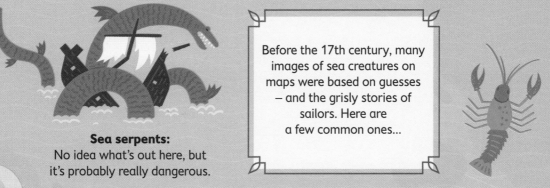

Before the 17th century, many images of sea creatures on maps were based on guesses – and the grisly stories of sailors. Here are a few common ones...

Sea serpents: No idea what's out here, but it's probably really dangerous.

Gigantic octopuses: We've heard stories of HUGE octopuses that will pull sailors overboard. We mapmakers like showing them as lobsters.

Whales: Whales have been seen here. These huge monsters can drag your ship down to the depths. Also, they might eat you.

Sea creatures: There are chickens, pigs and cows on land, so there are probably ocean-dwelling versions of these on the high seas.

Mermaids:
This area appears safe and calm but looks can be deceiving. There are hidden dangers everywhere.

Sometimes illustrations were used to show whether an area was considered safe or dangerous.

Ichthyocentaur: Part fish, part horse, part man – but entirely harmless. This area is as safe as it gets on the open sea. You shouldn't have any trouble here.

As scientific understanding of the world grew, sea monsters began to disappear from maps.

Maps were still illustrated, but the images served different purposes.

Whales: Whales are not as dangerous as we once thought. Their presence here means this is a good place to catch fish.

Sailing ship:
Just a decorative sailing ship.

King riding a sea monster:
This is a political statement. This part of the sea belongs to us. We are a powerful kingdom and have mastered the waves and their dangers.

33 The boat-house of lobsters...

was just one of many Norse names for the sea.

Over a thousand years ago, the sea was such a crucial part of Scandinavian life, that Old Norse poetry has more than 200 ways to describe the sea.

I need another name for the sea. Ideas anyone?

The plain of puffins, the land of salmon, the necklace of the Earth...

The whale road, the land of the ship, the water monsters' stronghold...

How about the enclosure of seaweed? The salty path of the keel, the otter world, the field of ice floes...

I've got some good names for ships: wave charger, horse of the sea, surf chariot, sea wolf, ski of the deep...

34 There's something fishy...

about the seafood on sale.

Passing off one kind of fish for another is a crime known as **seafood fraud**. The crime is so rife, recent studies have revealed that up to 30% of ALL seafood isn't what it says on the label.

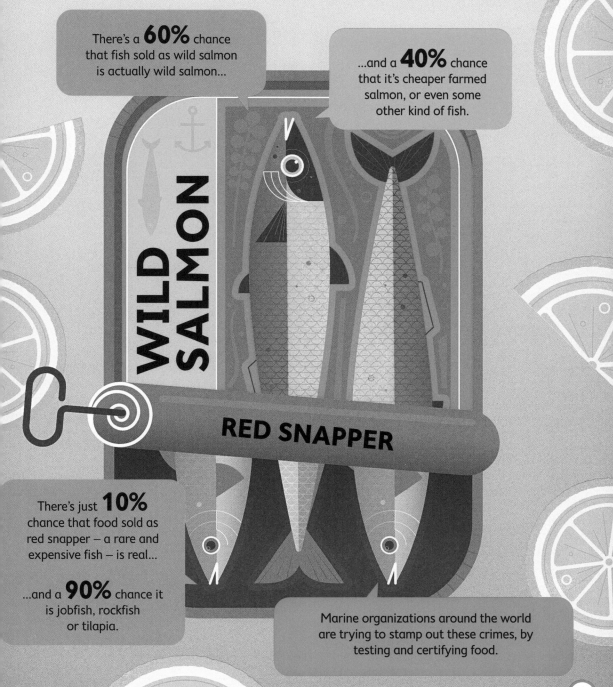

There's a **60%** chance that fish sold as wild salmon is actually wild salmon...

...and a **40%** chance that it's cheaper farmed salmon, or even some other kind of fish.

WILD SALMON

RED SNAPPER

There's just **10%** chance that food sold as red snapper – a rare and expensive fish – is real...

...and a **90%** chance it is jobfish, rockfish or tilapia.

Marine organizations around the world are trying to stamp out these crimes, by testing and certifying food.

on the mean streets of Kelp Forest.

Giant kelp is a type of seaweed that forms vast underwater forests in cool, shallow waters around the world. The forests provide food and shelter for thousands of species, but they're under attack, and an unlikely hero has come to the rescue...

Kelp Forest, USA...

...it used to be a paradise, where creatures lived in harmony.

We otters used to run this place.

Sea urchins kept to the shadows. They ate scraps of kelp — and we ate the sea urchins.

Everything was kept in *balance*.

But then came the Great Otter Hunt.

The humans killed us by the hundreds for our thick fur.

By 1820, the humans had *destroyed* our population.

Without otters, the sea urchins took over...

...and the forest became known as the Urchin Barrens.

MUNCH

SKRITCH

C'mon boys! Let's get that kelp!

MUNCH

Eat it all up!

SKRITCH

SKRITCH

MUNCH

SKRITCH

By the early 1900s, the humans finally realized their mistake and called off the hunt.

There's a lot to be done, but as our population recovers and grows, so too does the kelp forest.

36 Castle Bravo...

was a bomb dropped on paradise.

In the 1940s and 50s, after the Second World War, the USA tested powerful nuclear weapons in a remote area of the Pacific Ocean, near an island called the Bikini Atoll. One test – *"Castle Bravo"* – was one of the largest detonations in history...

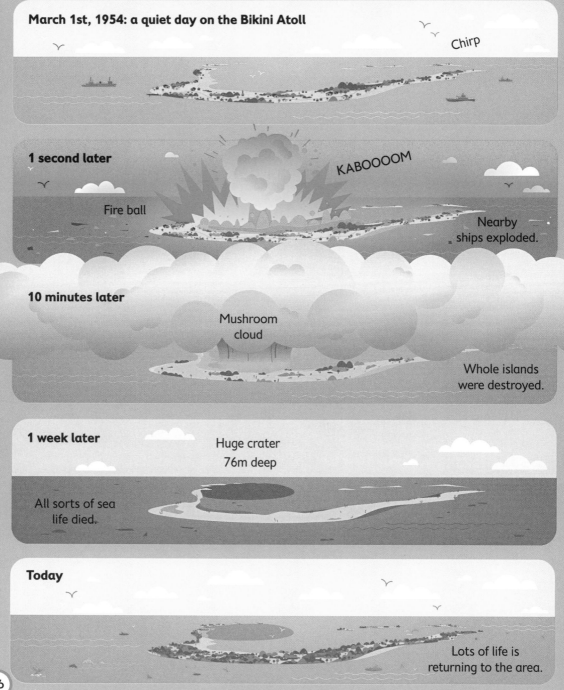

March 1st, 1954: a quiet day on the Bikini Atoll

Chirp

1 second later

KABOOOOM

Fire ball

Nearby ships exploded.

10 minutes later

Mushroom cloud

Whole islands were destroyed.

1 week later

Huge crater 76m deep

All sorts of sea life died.

Today

Lots of life is returning to the area.

37 Mutant crabs...

thrive on radioactive coconuts.

The bombs dropped on the Bikini Atoll were made of dangerous, long-lasting materials. They contaminated the whole area, making it unsafe for people to live there, even today.

People were evacuated from the Bikini Atoll and all the nearby islands during the 1940s and 50s. They're still not allowed to go back.

But despite the devastation, over the last 50 years, the reef has filled back up with life. Not only is life managing to survive there, it's thriving.

The seas are full of fish, sharks, huge corals and crabs the size of hub caps – despite the fact they consume contaminated food and water, including the coconuts that grow on the atoll.

There is so much thriving life precisely *because* there are no people around to disturb or hunt the creatures.

38 You can *feel* an island...

before you *see* one.

For thousands of years, people living on Pacific islands made long voyages across the ocean. They set their course by the position of the Sun and stars – but they also used other clues, such as soaring birds, towering clouds and the feel of the waves beneath their boats.

Even without modern compasses, charts and satellite technology, these navigators could find their way from one island to another across thousands of miles of ocean.

Here's how they did it.

1

By memorizing stars
Navigators learned the positions of hundreds of stars. They knew where each appeared on the horizon at night, and how it moved across the sky. This told them which direction they were sailing in.

2

By tracking the Sun
The Sun rises in the East and sets in the West.

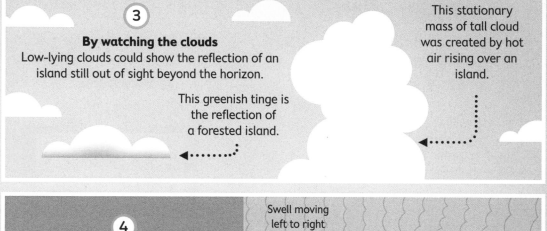

3

By watching the clouds
Low-lying clouds could show the reflection of an island still out of sight beyond the horizon.

This stationary mass of tall cloud was created by hot air rising over an island.

This greenish tinge is the reflection of a forested island.

4

By feeling nearby islands
Ocean waves called swells bend around and bounce off islands. This makes distinct patterns of waves that navigators could feel beneath their boat — even when the island was still 50km (31 miles) away.

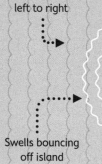

Swell moving left to right

Swells bouncing off island

Overlapping swell pattern

5

By counting fins
A rise in the number of animals such as sharks and dolphins showed that land was nearby.

6

By watching the birds
Some birds, such as terns and noddies, return to land every evening after a day's fishing. They could show the way to a nearby island.

7

By watching a pig
On long journeys, navigators often sailed with livestock on board. Pigs have a keen sense of smell, and when they caught the scent of an island, they pointed their noses toward it.

39 A deep-sea explorer...

made her biggest discovery on dry land.

For centuries, people thought the sea floor was a flat, muddy plain. But in the 1950s, scientist Marie Tharp discovered all manner of underwater ridges, canyons and peaks – all without setting foot on a boat.

Tharp was a geologist who worked with a team of scientists to explore the ocean floor.

The team used a ship to measure the ocean's depth in thousands of different places...

...but Tharp wasn't allowed on board the vessel, as women weren't permitted to join the crew.

In her New York office, she studied the team's data and transformed it into maps. These revealed unexpected features, such as a deep trench running through a mountain range in the Atlantic Ocean.

13442 ft 13440 ft
13435 ft 13418 ft
13400 ft 13399 ft
13432 ft 13439 ft
13451 ft 13457 ft

Tharp was the first to realize that this was where two large sections of the Earth's crust – called **tectonic plates** – are slowly drifting apart.

Her work helped shape our understanding of how the planet fits together.

40 Titan has waterless seas...

and sandless shores.

Spacecraft flying past Titan (Saturn's largest moon) have found rivers, lakes and even seas. In fact, Titan resembles Earth more closely than anything we've found in space – except that its seas aren't made of water...

Spot the difference

Snow made of frozen water

Snow made of frozen benzene*

Sea made of liquid salt water

Sea made of liquid ethane* and methane*

Dunes made of sand grains

Dunes made of frozen grains of ethane

*Benzene, ethane and methane are highly flammable chemicals made from hydrogen and carbon. They are used to make fuels for cars and other machinery.

41 Underwater supervillains...

come in every size and shape.

What is the most dangerous sea creature you can imagine? A great white shark? A killer whale? Or what about something much, much smaller? Some creatures living in coral reefs have developed abilities so amazing – and deadly – they could be described as superpowers.

BLUE-RINGED OCTOPUS

- Has enough venom in its bite to kill 26 humans
- Camouflage skin changes to match its surroundings
- Flashes purple rings as a warning when threatened
- Uses jets to speed through water

VENOM

SECRET SUPERPOWER:
Stealth bite (you won't even know you've been bitten)

GREATEST WEAKNESS:
Small size: 12-20cm (5-8in)

YELLOW-LIPPED SEA KRAIT

- Black and white stripes warn off predators
- Can move on land and sea
- Its paddle-shaped tail makes it a swift swimmer
- Has a powerful venomous bite

VENOM

SECRET SUPERPOWER:
Can always find its way home

GREATEST WEAKNESS:
Often gets tangled in fishing nets

RED LIONFISH

- Brightly patterned mane of spines serves as a warning: don't mess with me!
- Spines are venomous
- Aggressive hunter

VENOM
○ ○ ● ● ●

SECRET SUPERPOWER:
Big gulp (swallows prey whole)

GREATEST WEAKNESS:
Tastes delicious

In brightest bay, in darkest reef, our powers seem beyond belief!

GEOGRAPHY CONE SNAIL

- Protected by a thick shell
- Burrows in sand for sneak attacks
- Shoots a barbed harpoon that injects victims with venom
- Has the most venomous sting in the world – with no known cure

VENOM
● ● ● ● ●

SECRET SUPERPOWER:
Super sense of smell detects prey

GREATEST WEAKNESS:
Can't move very quickly

53

42 Specks of plastic in the ocean...

outnumber the stars in the Milky Way.

Our solar system is part of the **Milky Way galaxy**: a vast, swirling disk of dust, planets and up to **400 billion** stars. That may seem like a lot...

...but the Earth's oceans are polluted by many TRILLIONS of pieces of plastic.

This plastic waste can last for hundreds of years, slowly leaking chemicals and poisoning animals that swallow it.

Much of it is made up of **microplastics**: specks of plastic less than **5mm (0.2 inches)** across. These often form when larger pieces of litter break down over time.

Like twinkling stars, microplastics *seem* small.

But in fact there are so many that we may never clean them up. The only way to fight this HUGE PROBLEM is to use less plastic.

43 This page is covered in...

seaweed.

Whether it's wrapped around sushi rice, cooked in a stir-fry or tossed in a salad, humans have eaten seaweed for thousands of years. In fact, we put it in all sorts of things, and it can be found on our shelves in lots of unexpected places...

Ketchup

Lipstick

Whipped cream

Seaweed contains substances called **agar**, **alginate** and **carrageenan**, which can be extracted and added to various products.

Yogurt

Toothpaste

Seaweed extracts are a natural way to thicken, stabilize and bind things together.

Soy and almond milk

Gravy

Chocolate milk

Medicines

Mayo

Salad dressing

Stops the milk and chocolate from separating

Paint

Keeps ice cream smooth

Chicken nuggets

Lotions

Frozen meat and fish

Pet food

Cakes

Soup

Stops oily fish from going bad

Pie and pastry fillings

Paper

44 Ghost nets...

haunt the seas long after they've been lost.

Fishing nets that have been lost or discarded at sea are known as **ghost nets**. A single ghost net can drift through the water for years, entangling and killing *thousands* of fish and other sea creatures.

Tens of thousands of miles of fishing nets end up in the sea every year due to accidents or carelessness.

Each can be up to 2.5km (1.5 miles) long, and they are nearly invisible underwater, making them almost impossible to avoid.

Worst of all, most are made of strong, long-lasting plastics, which won't break down for many decades.

45 Dead zones...

blot out underwater life.

Dead zones are areas in the ocean with so little oxygen that nothing can survive. They can occur naturally, but are increasingly caused by pollution from human activity, and can cover tens of thousands of miles.

Some farmers use chemical-rich fertilizers containing phosphorus and nitrogen to help their crops grow.

When water runs off the farm fields, it takes some of these chemicals with it, and they eventually end up in the ocean.

All these chemicals in the water cause the population of algae (a small, plant-like organism) to explode – covering the surface of the water in a green sludge.

When the algae dies, it sinks to the sea floor and begins to decompose. It sucks all the oxygen out of the water, making it impossible for anything to survive.

46 The secret to a long life...

is a good friendship.

Clownfish and certain sea anemones make the best buddies. They live together in coral reefs, where they help each other out in many ways.

We eat algae and tiny creatures on the anemone. Yum! This also keeps the anemone clean.

As we dart about, water flows between the anemone's tentacles, bringing it extra food. And anemones feed on our droppings too!

Anemones have stinging tentacles that protect us from predators. But slimy mucus on our bodies stops us from being stung.

If an anemone-eating butterfly fish comes near, we chase it away!

This friendship is an example of what scientists call symbiosis.

Living with anemones helps clownfish live for up to 20 years – that's four times longer than other fish their size.

THE OCEAN OBSERVER

SCIENTISTS DISCOVER DEEP–SEA "HOT TUB" THAT KILLS WHOEVER DARES TAKE A DIP

In the Gulf of Mexico, nearly 1,000m (3,300ft) below the surface, sits a super salty and toxic gas-filled brine pool, known as the hot tub of despair.

Local residents are clacking their claws and flapping their fins with distress over this warm but toxic gas-filled lake on the ocean floor.

Mussels live at the edge of the lake. Bacteria in their gills convert the toxic gases found in the lake into food.

A colony of mussels who live at the edge of the lake said, "Just glance over the surface and you can see it is littered with the shells of long-dead crabs and fish that have been pickled in its waters."

Despite the danger, there's something about the lake that continues to lure all manner of ocean dwellers to it...

☠ BUT WHAT IS A BRINE POOL? ☠

Brine pools form when the seabed shifts and ancient salt deposits are released into the surrounding water.

Being extra salty makes this water much heavier than regular sea water, so it sinks to the bottom.

Brine pools contain almost no oxygen, but lots of highly toxic chemicals such as methane gas. This is what makes it impossible for most animals to survive.

For this dangerous natural phenomenon, there's just one way to stay safe – stay OUT.

48 Coastguard, cleaner, nanny...
mangrove trees can do it all.

THE OCEAN OBSERVER JOBS PAGES

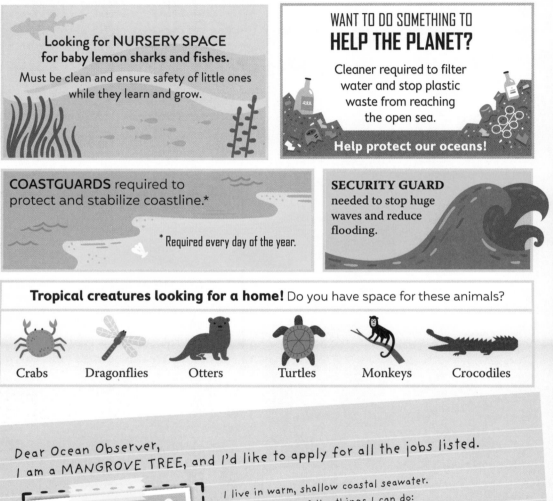

Looking for NURSERY SPACE for baby lemon sharks and fishes.

Must be clean and ensure safety of little ones while they learn and grow.

WANT TO DO SOMETHING TO
HELP THE PLANET?

Cleaner required to filter water and stop plastic waste from reaching the open sea.

Help protect our oceans!

COASTGUARDS required to protect and stabilize coastline.*

* Required every day of the year.

SECURITY GUARD needed to stop huge waves and reduce flooding.

Tropical creatures looking for a home! Do you have space for these animals?

| Crabs | Dragonflies | Otters | Turtles | Monkeys | Crocodiles |

Dear Ocean Observer,
I am a MANGROVE TREE, and I'd like to apply for all the jobs listed.

Mangrove Tree

I live in warm, shallow coastal seawater.
Here are some of the things I can do:
- I have big roots like stilts that CAN SHELTER CREATURES and act like a NURSERY.
- My roots CATCH PLASTIC WASTE so it can be easily picked up.
- I can CLEAN AND FILTER WATER.
- My roots STABILIZE SHORES and coastlines, and PROTECT THEM FROM FLOODING.
- My leaves, branches, roots, fruits and flowers can HOUSE THOUSANDS OF SPECIES.

49 Parrotfish wear PJs...

made of mucus.

When night falls in coral reefs around the world, tropical fish called parrotfish slowly wrap themselves in a onesie made from their own mucus. Then, once they're safely tucked in, they go to sleep.

The parrotfishes' main night-time predator is the **moray eel**.

Moray eels can't see well, so they rely on their sense of smell to locate prey.

Scientists think the mucus PJs mask the parrotfishes' scent, so that the eels can't detect them.

The mucus also keeps off tiny pests and parasites that could disturb the parrotfish in their sleep.

50 Phantom islands...

only exist on paper.

Sea charts have long included errors called **phantom islands**: islands that early explorers discovered and added to their maps – but which later proved *not* to exist. So, what made sailors think they'd discovered new islands? Breaking waves, tricks of light and floating debris could all look like land from the deck of a ship.

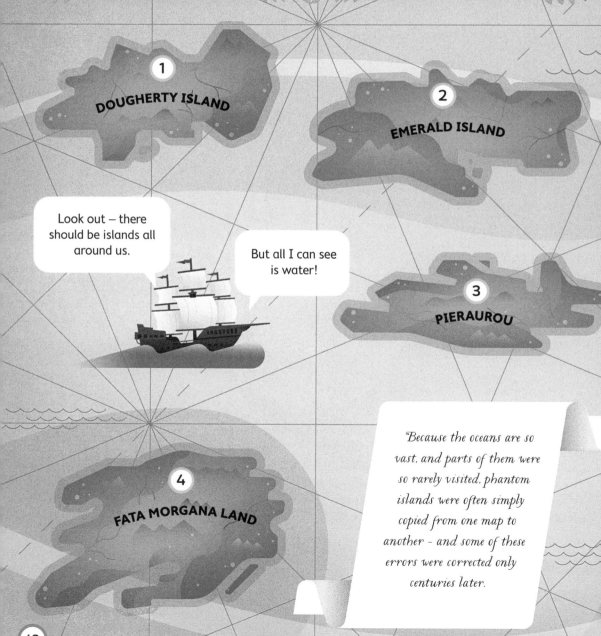

1 DOUGHERTY ISLAND

2 EMERALD ISLAND

3 PIERAUROU

4 FATA MORGANA LAND

Look out – there should be islands all around us.

But all I can see is water!

Because the oceans are so vast, and parts of them were so rarely visited, phantom islands were often simply copied from one map to another - and some of these errors were corrected only centuries later.

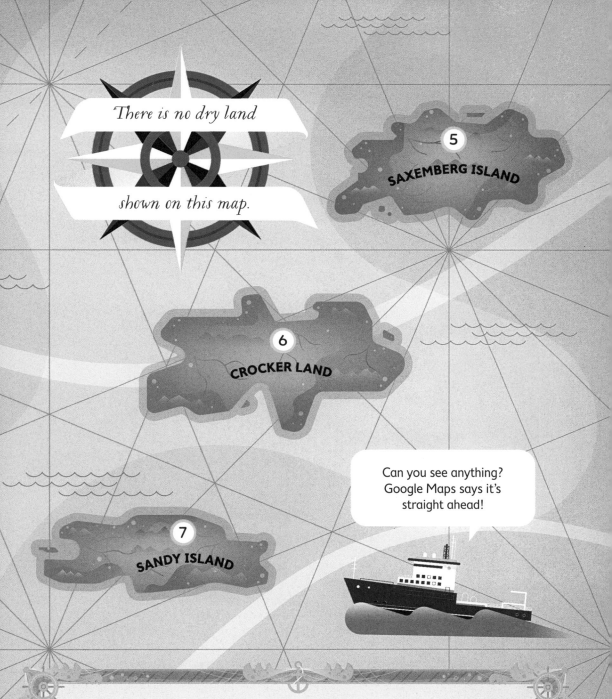

There is no dry land

shown on this map.

5 SAXEMBERG ISLAND

6 CROCKER LAND

Can you see anything? Google Maps says it's straight ahead!

7 SANDY ISLAND

Although this is a made-up map, the names of the islands on it are real. None of them actually exist, but at some point in the last 400 years, people *thought* they did.

These "islands" were probably just...

1) An iceberg. 2) A looming bank of fog. 3) A submerged bank of sand.
4) An optical illusion. 5) Real – but temporary. This island probably *did* exist for a time, but was destroyed by a volcanic eruption. 6) A hoax – invented by an explorer seeking fame and fortune. 7) A raft of floating volcanic stone. Sandy Island actually featured on some maps right up until 2012.

51 Paper fishes...

reveal secrets of the ocean's past.

For hundreds of years, Japanese fishermen have recorded prize catches by making inked fish prints called *gyotaku*. These prints aren't just a valued art form: they can also teach scientists about what once swam beneath the waves.

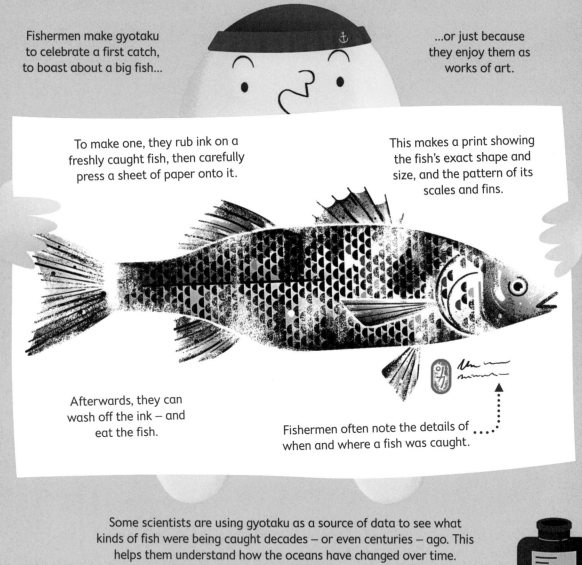

Fishermen make gyotaku to celebrate a first catch, to boast about a big fish...

...or just because they enjoy them as works of art.

To make one, they rub ink on a freshly caught fish, then carefully press a sheet of paper onto it.

This makes a print showing the fish's exact shape and size, and the pattern of its scales and fins.

Afterwards, they can wash off the ink — and eat the fish.

Fishermen often note the details of when and where a fish was caught.

Some scientists are using gyotaku as a source of data to see what kinds of fish were being caught decades — or even centuries — ago. This helps them understand how the oceans have changed over time.

52 A *steel beach picnic...*

is a barbecue on the deck of a submarine or ship.

Some navy submarines stay underwater for several months at a time, only surfacing to replenish food supplies. But occasionally, a submarine surfaces and the captain authorizes a picnic on deck and a swim.

A chef cooks burgers on a grill on the deck.

Lookouts scan the ocean for sharks.

Life on board a submarine can be boring and tense, so events like this help to cheer up the submariners.

53 Marine snow...

falls mainly in the summer.

On the seabed, all is cold, dark and still – except for millions of white flakes drifting softly down, slowly piling into drifts. This is marine snow, and in many parts of the ocean, it's a sure sign that summer is here.

Marine snow is made up of debris sinking down from the surface...

...such as dust, sand, droppings from sea creatures...

...and especially, the remains of **phytoplankton** – tiny plants that grow in sunny surface waters.

In many places, phytoplankton multiply in the spring and die off in the summer, causing an extra-heavy snowfall.

54 The loneliest whale...

sings a song no one else can understand.

In the 1980s, scientists began picking up undersea recordings of a whale singing. They'd heard whale song before, but this particular whale's song didn't resemble any other ever heard.

Whales make sounds to communicate with each other. The sounds travel in **waves** of high or low **frequency**.

A squashed-up wave like this is a high frequency, which makes a high sound.

A stretched-out wave like this is a low frequency, which makes a low sound.

Frequency is measured in **hertz** (Hz).

Blue whale sounds: between 10 and 40Hz

Fin whale sounds: 20Hz

But this individual whale sang at **52Hz** – and it doesn't seem to belong to a recognized species.

Scientists have been tracking this "52Hz whale" for 30 years. Its frequency has actually been dropping, and it is now singing at around 47Hz, but it's still never been seen...

Scientists aren't sure what kind of whale it is, or why it makes this sound. It may be deaf, or have a uniquely shaped head.

55 The Bloop...

is one of the loudest sounds ever recorded.

In 1997, underwater microphones picked up one of the loudest sounds researchers had ever come across. Nicknamed *the Bloop*, it baffled scientists for years...

It was originally thought to have come from a massive, unknown species of whale, or a kind of giant squid.

The Bloop was **ultra low frequency** – too low for human ears to hear.

The Bloop

Years later, in 2005, researchers finally discovered the source: it was caused by a colossal block of ice breaking under the sea, sending a loud rumble across 3,000km (1,850 miles).

56 Some sharks don't grow up...

for 150 years.

Living in the icy cold waters of the Arctic and North Atlantic Oceans slows the growth and aging of Greenland sharks so dramatically that they can live for a really, *really* long time.

No you can't stay up that late. You're only 147 years old!

Greenland sharks mature so slowly that they're not even considered to be grown-ups until they reach an adult length of around 4m (13ft) at

150

years of age.

Just a few years ago, scientists found a Greenland shark in the North Atlantic. It was 5m (16ft) long, and the scientists estimated it was around **400** years old.

57 A tsunami can outpace...

a racing car or bullet train.

Tsunamis are huge ocean waves, usually triggered by earthquakes below the seabed. The waves can travel through the ocean for hundreds of miles before striking land – and they do it at an astonishing speed.

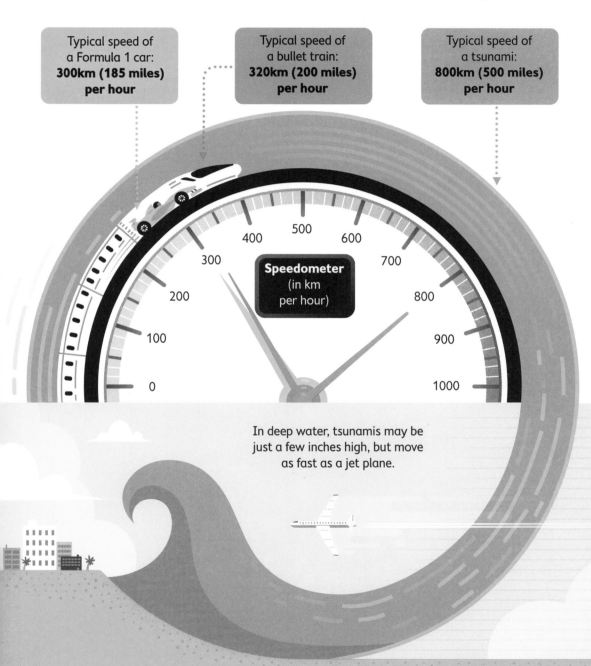

Typical speed of a Formula 1 car: **300km (185 miles) per hour**

Typical speed of a bullet train: **320km (200 miles) per hour**

Typical speed of a tsunami: **800km (500 miles) per hour**

Speedometer (in km per hour)

In deep water, tsunamis may be just a few inches high, but move as fast as a jet plane.

When they reach the shallow water of a coast, the slope of the sea floor pushes the waves up out of the depths. This slows them down – but they can reach colossal heights.

58 Millions of Dutch people...

live under water.

Nearly one third of the Netherlands, in Europe, lies below sea level. Living among lakes, rivers and bogs, with the North Sea licking the dunes, the Dutch have always faced the risk of deadly floods.

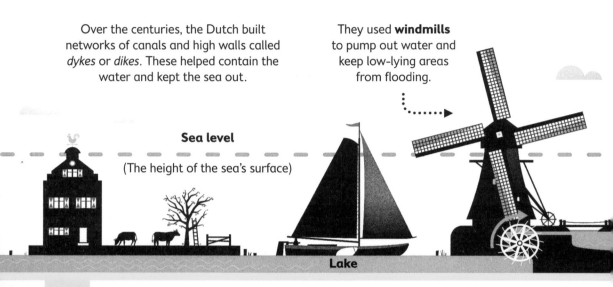

Over the centuries, the Dutch built networks of canals and high walls called *dykes* or *dikes*. These helped contain the water and kept the sea out.

They used **windmills** to pump out water and keep low-lying areas from flooding.

Sea level

(The height of the sea's surface)

Lake

59 Underwater skate parks...

can combat rising sea levels.

Today, higher temperatures are melting the planet's ice caps and slowly raising sea levels. Building higher dykes isn't a guarantee against future floods. So instead, the Dutch are redesigning their cities.

Extreme storms are rare — but when they come, they can push the sea over walls and barriers, causing catastrophic flooding.

Floating houses — built on foundations made from lightweight materials, can rise and fall with floodwaters.

North Sea

Flood waters ......

Canal

The windmills worked in groups, each one driving a wheel that scooped up water as it turned, lifting it to a higher level.

After passing up in stages from canal to canal, the water was pumped out into the sea.

The same system is still used today – but with modern pumps, powered by fuel or electricity, rather than windmills.

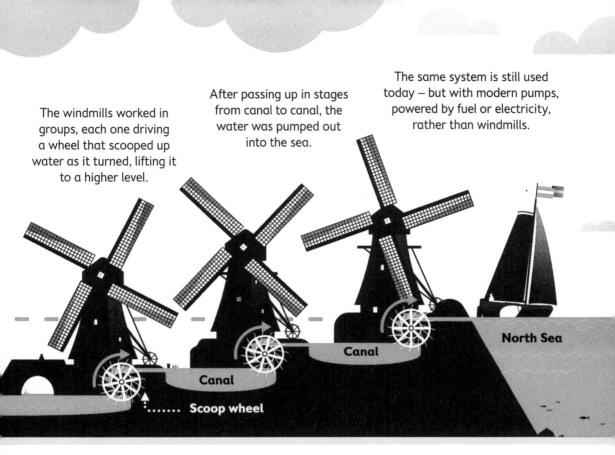

North Sea

Canal

Canal

········ **Scoop wheel**

Public plazas called **water squares** are built down into the ground – lower than the buildings around them.

During extreme storms or floods, water can drain into the empty square rather than into nearby homes.

On the low-lying ground most likely to flood, the Dutch build skate parks, playgrounds and nature reserves.

By creating more space for floodwaters, the Dutch hope to keep their cities safe in a warming world.

Skate park

Water square

60 The luckiest castaways...

landed on islands near New Zealand.

In the 1800s, ships were regularly wrecked on the many barren, uninhabited islands to the south of New Zealand. Eventually, the government set up special huts there, called **castaway depots**, to provide survivors with food and shelter until they could be rescued.

WELCOME TO NEW ZEALAND'S SUBANTARCTIC ISLANDS

Things could be worse!

Stay in a rustic castaway depot...

Follow the finger post signs to your own snug little hut, where you'll find everything you need to weather wind and storms.

The castaway depots were used until the late 1920s. Then, thanks to better charts and navigation equipment, and stronger, safer ships, shipwrecks became much rarer.

Keep warm in blustery weather...

Depots are stocked with woollen blankets and clothing woven with a distinctive pattern, meant to deter thieves.

Enjoy a balanced diet...

Menus include

Free range pork, lamb and beef
(Islands are stocked with animals to hunt and eat)

Freshly caught fish
(If you catch it yourself)

An extensive selection of tinned foods
(Especially beans!)

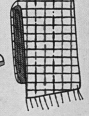

Try a wide range of activities...

All depots contain hunting rifles, fishhooks and fishing lines.

Selected depots have a boat for recreation — or for transportation to other islands and depots nearby.

On rainy days, try making your own chess board, or carve your name into the side of your bunk.

Maximum stay: six months

Don't get too settled into island life. A steamship visits each depot twice a year to replenish supplies and rescue any castaways.

61 Godzilla, Mothra, Sasquatch...

stand tall on the Pacific floor.

In the 1980s, deep-sea submersibles took pictures of smoke-spewing monsters that loomed in the darkness. Scientists identified them as **hydrothermal vents** – rock formations like deep-sea volcanoes. They named several vents after monsters from film and legend.

The vents, also known as **black smokers**, shoot out billowing thick black dust and water that can reach over **460°C (860°F)** – hot enough to melt lead.

In the cold of the ocean, some of the dust cools rapidly and sticks to the vents, making them taller.

Mothra

Godzilla

Sasquatch

The vent named Godzilla grew to more than

50m (164ft)

– before most of it toppled onto the ocean floor.

Since then it has begun to grow back, sometimes by more than **5m (15ft)** in a single year.

62 Sulfur-guzzling tube worms...

eat with no mouths or stomachs.

Among the extreme heat and smoke of hydrothermal vents, researchers have found abundant life. Rather than feeding on plants and animals, one life form in this hostile environment feeds on the sulfur gas that spews out from many vents. They're called giant tube worms.

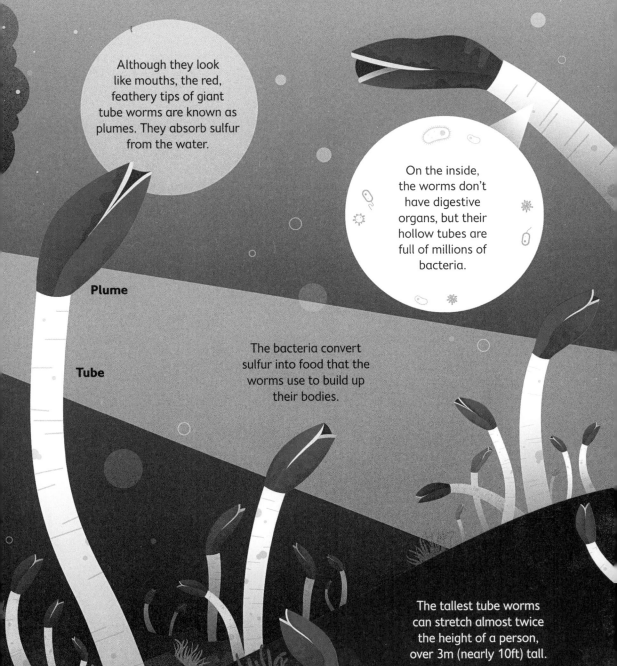

Although they look like mouths, the red, feathery tips of giant tube worms are known as plumes. They absorb sulfur from the water.

On the inside, the worms don't have digestive organs, but their hollow tubes are full of millions of bacteria.

Plume

Tube

The bacteria convert sulfur into food that the worms use to build up their bodies.

The tallest tube worms can stretch almost twice the height of a person, over 3m (nearly 10ft) tall.

63 Thirst is the worst...

for people lost at sea.

When disaster hits, and people are lost at sea, they face three great threats. As it happens, the scariest of these is actually the least likely...

If their body loses more water than it takes in, it's called **dehydration**. In time, it can stop them from breathing.

Sea water is so salty it will dehydrate me faster than drinking nothing at all.

1 THIRST

If their blood temperature drops below 35°C (95°F), it's called **hypothermia**. This can stop their hearts from beating.

2 COLD

3 SHARKS

I'll try not to worry about sharks — it's very, VERY unlikely that one will find me, let alone try to eat me.

There isn't a medical term for being eaten by a shark, obviously, but it would be fatal.

If I curl up into a ball, I can stay warm for longer.

On a small boat or raft, people can survive at sea for months by drinking rainwater and catching fish. Even alone in the open water, people have survived more than 30 hours before being rescued.

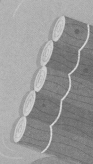

On the 13th of August, 1896, a ship called the *Fram* sailed out of dense polar ice near the islands of Svalbard. It had spent three years exploring the Arctic – surviving where countless other ships had sunk.

At the time, most ships had deep hulls with straight sides: good for sailing...

Crrreak! *Crrrack!*

...but easily caught and crushed between the huge plates of ice that surrounded ships in the Arctic.

To avoid being crushed, Norwegian explorer Fridtjof Nansen built a ship to be stronger, rounder and slippery.

Whoop!

It had a shallow profile shaped like the bottom of an egg. When squeezed by ice, the ship would just slip up out of its grip.

Windmill to power electric lights

Safe inside the *Fram*, Nansen and his crew spent many months drifting along *on top of* the Arctic ice.

Layers of felt, shaved cork and reindeer hair to keep out the cold

Multiple layers of hardwood planks

Thanks to its egg-shaped design, the *Fram* would survive many Arctic and Antarctic expeditions.

65 Migrating woodpeckers...

make tiger shark snacks.

Many birds that live inland, including woodpeckers, wrens and warblers, fly huge distances across oceans twice a year. As they fly, some birds get blown into the water, where tiger sharks are ready to gobble them up.

Each spring, two billion birds cross the Gulf of Mexico between Mexico and the USA.

Then, from September to October, they fly back again.

And, during each journey, tiger sharks gather beneath their flight paths.

Birds that live inland don't have oily feathers like seabirds, and cannot survive long if they tire and fall into the water...

...making them easy prey for the waiting sharks.

66 To find sunken treasure...

you need a good lawyer.

The treasure found in ancient shipwrecks can be worth billions. But if you discover a sunken treasure ship on the ocean floor, is it yours to keep? The question is often decided by long and costly lawsuits, or court cases.

It is common for several countries and organizations to claim part, or all, of a valuable wreck.

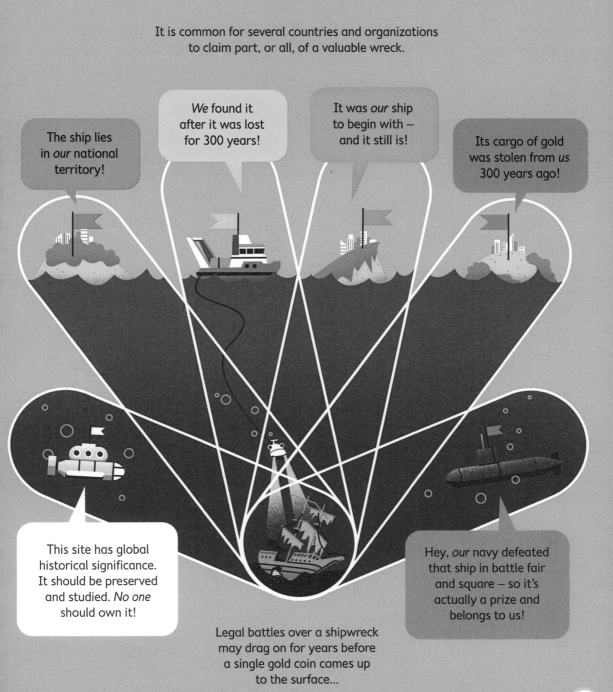

The ship lies in *our* national territory!

We found it after it was lost for 300 years!

It was *our* ship to begin with – and it still is!

Its cargo of gold was stolen from *us* 300 years ago!

This site has global historical significance. It should be preserved and studied. *No one* should own it!

Hey, *our* navy defeated that ship in battle fair and square – so it's actually a prize and belongs to us!

Legal battles over a shipwreck may drag on for years before a single gold coin comes up to the surface...

The oceans boiled...

billions of years ago.

The Earth was formed 4.6 billion years ago, as a swirling mass of hot rock and fire. Many scientists think that, by 4 billion years ago, liquid oceans had appeared on the planet – even though temperatures were a blistering 230°C (460°F) on the surface.

At that temperature, water should turn to steam and evaporate into the air...

...but scientists think high pressure pushing down on the ocean from the atmosphere kept the water liquid.

So, for thousands of years, the oceans *literally boiled*.

Scientists call this the Hadean era, after Hades, Greek god of the underworld, because of the fiery conditions.

It wasn't for many more millions of years that the Earth cooled, and the oceans looked as they do today.

68 Listening to a radio code...

keeps sailors safe at sea.

Every day, the UK's BBC Radio broadcasts its *Shipping Forecast*, describing the conditions at sea around the British Isles. Announcers squeeze essential information into just 370 words, by using a set of specific phrases that act like a code understood by seafarers.

Forties[1]: Backing[2], Violent storm[3] Imminent[4], Phenomenal[5], Poor.[6]

Each list begins with the name of one of 31 listed locations followed by further details.

(1) Location

(2) Wind direction

Veering	moving clockwise
Backing	moving anti- or counterclockwise
Cyclonic	considerable change in direction

(3) Gale warning – wind force

Gale	force 8
Storm	force 10
Violent storm	force 11

(4) Gale warning timing

Imminent	within 6 hours
Soon	6 - 12 hours
Later	after 12 hours

(5) Sea state – wave height

Smooth	less than 0.5m (1.6ft)
Moderate	1.25 - 2.5m (4.1 - 8.2ft)
Rough	2.5 - 4m (8.2 - 13.1ft)
High	6 - 9m (19.7 - 29.5ft)
Phenomenal	more than 14m (46ft)

(6) Visibility – how far you can see

Visibility is calculated in **nautical miles (nm)** – a unit of distance equal to 1,852m or 6,076ft

Good	more than 5 nm
Moderate	2 to 5 nm
Poor	1km (3,200ft) to 2 nm
Very poor	less than 1km (3,200ft)

Inspired by the BBC, countries around the world use a similar system in their own languages.

69 Libraries of sand and rock...

tell the story of the ocean.

Around the world, scientific institutes hold vast collections of samples drilled out from below the seabed, known as **cores**. Examining these cores helps scientists to build up a picture of how water has flowed around the oceans at different times in the past.

> Pass me a sample of south Atlantic from 2003, would you please?

> Hold on, I'm just sorting through the northwest Pacific from 1968.

> Most cores show distinct layers. The top layer here is the most recent. It shows that the seabed was mostly made of shells at the time this core was drilled.

Mostly shells   Mostly limestone   Mostly sandstone

Each layer shows what the seabed was like at different times in past centuries.

Sometimes cores taken from different oceans can have matching layers, showing that water flowed from one ocean into another.

70 Some lifeboats sink...
before they float.

All large ships carry lifeboats to transport the crew to safety in case of emergency. Conventional lifeboats are lowered on cables or ropes from the ship to the sea, but this takes time – sometimes *too much* time.

Some vessels, such as oil tankers, can catch fire and explode. Instead of conventional lifeboats, they carry **freefall lifeboats**, specially designed to evacuate the crew rapidly.

If disaster strikes, the ship's crew scramble aboard the lifeboat and strap themselves in.

Then, the lifeboat slides down a track and plummets to the sea below...

ATALA
LONDO

The lifeboats can safely fall up to **50m (164 feet)** and hit the water at a speed of up to **110km (70 miles) per hour**.

...plunging in and sinking beneath the waves...

...before bobbing up a short distance away, ready to speed off to safety.

71 Gloomy octopuses...

have built an underwater city.

Octopuses prefer to spend their lives alone. But one species, the gloomy octopus, might not be as solitary as scientists once thought. Below the waves in Jervis Bay, Australia, sits a sought-after patch of ocean floor nicknamed Octopolis.

Marine biologists studying Octopolis have observed the octopuses...

1 ...living together

What kind of home are you looking for? Sand? Shells?

2 ...chasing unwelcome octopuses away

Get out of here Chad!

Crime Watch

Welcome to Octopolis: the most exclusive homes south of the Equator!

When it was discovered in 2009, Octopolis was the first place scientists had ever found octopuses living together. Then, in 2017, marine biologists discovered a second site nearby, which they named Octlantis.

72 Zooplankton commute...

each and every day.

Each morning, trillions of microscopic creatures called **zooplankton** journey down into deep ocean. Each evening, they come back to the surface. By mass, it's the biggest migration - movement of a large group of creatures – on the planet. And they do it every day.

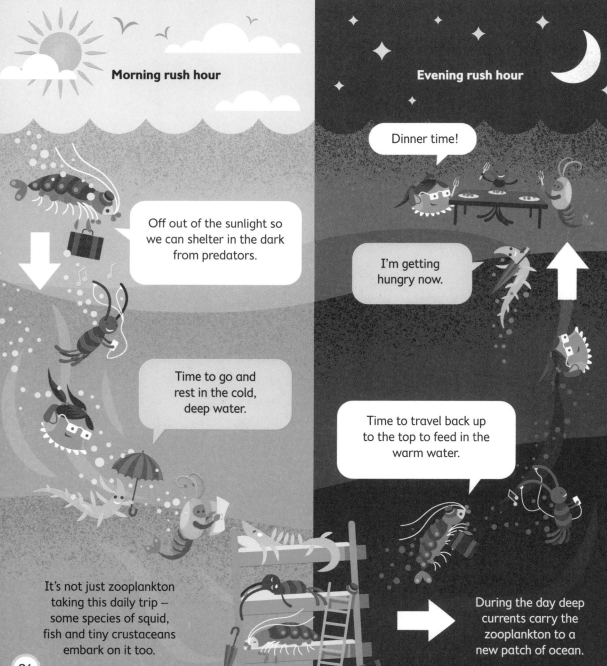

Morning rush hour

Evening rush hour

Dinner time!

Off out of the sunlight so we can shelter in the dark from predators.

I'm getting hungry now.

Time to go and rest in the cold, deep water.

Time to travel back up to the top to feed in the warm water.

It's not just zooplankton taking this daily trip – some species of squid, fish and tiny crustaceans embark on it too.

During the day deep currents carry the zooplankton to a new patch of ocean.

73 A good kayak...
should fit like a tailored suit.

For thousands of years, native people in the Arctic region used kayaks – lightweight, one-person boats – to hunt and fish. Each kayak was made to measure, and tailored to fit one individual paddler.

A traditional kayak should be three times the length of the paddler's outstretched arms.

Its cockpit, where the paddler sits, should be their width plus two fists.

Inside, the boat should be as deep as the paddler's fist, plus an outstretched thumb.

A kayak is made from thin pieces of driftwood, antler and whalebone, pierced with holes and sewn together into a lightweight frame.

Sealskins are stretched over the frame, sewn together, and rubbed with whale fat to make the boat waterproof.

If a kayak is properly fitted, it's more stable, more agile, easier to paddle, and lets in less cold Arctic water.

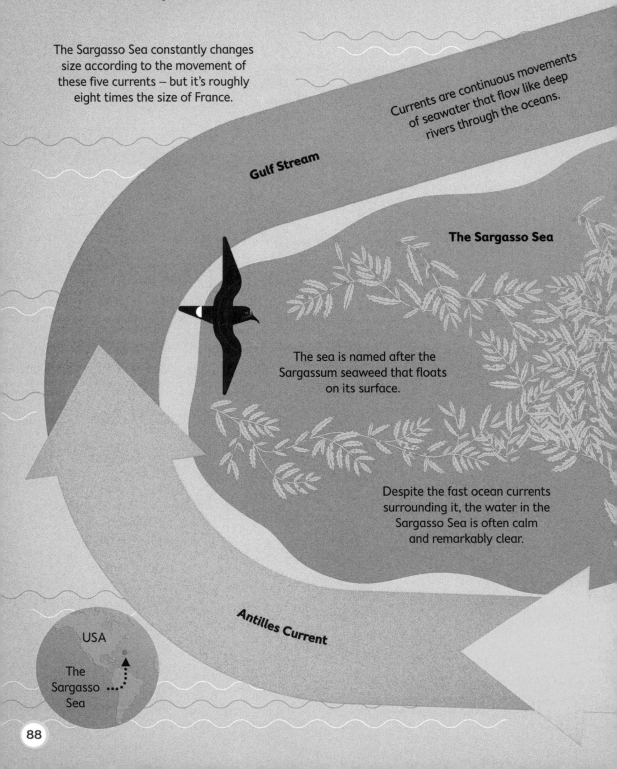

74 The only sea without a shore...

is the Sargasso Sea.

The Sargasso Sea lies within the Atlantic Ocean, east of Bermuda. It is bounded by ocean currents that swirl, clockwise, around it.

The Sargasso Sea constantly changes size according to the movement of these five currents — but it's roughly eight times the size of France.

Currents are continuous movements of seawater that flow like deep rivers through the oceans.

Gulf Stream

The Sargasso Sea

The sea is named after the Sargassum seaweed that floats on its surface.

Despite the fast ocean currents surrounding it, the water in the Sargasso Sea is often calm and remarkably clear.

Antilles Current

USA

The Sargasso Sea

Azores Current

Sargassum weed provides protection and food for many creatures, including white marlin, porbeagle sharks and newly hatched eels.

Canary Current

Young loggerhead turtles hide from predators in the weeds. The weeds absorb sunlight and help the turtles stay warm, so they can feed and grow faster.

North Equatorial Current

Underwater lights...

dazzle, startle, seduce and confuse.

Lots of sea creatures are **bioluminescent**, meaning their bodies produce light. The light does different jobs in different species...

Some species contain fluorescent chemicals that glow under certain conditions. In others, the light is made by bacteria living inside the creature.

Angler fish

Jellyfish

Attracting prey

Anglerfish lure little fish into their open mouths, with a light called an esca on the end of a stem called an illicium.

Confusing predators

Lots of jellyfish are bioluminescent. Some glow green or blue when they're disturbed, to dazzle a predator.

Bristlemouth

Dragonfish

Firefly squid

Camouflaging

Bristlemouth fish have a row of lights along their underside. For any predators looking up, this makes them blend in with the bright sky above.

Seeing in the dark

Barbeled dragonfish glow red. This allows them to see – and eat – little red creatures that would be otherwise invisible in dark, deep water.

Startling predators

If firefly squid are attacked, they squirt out a big cloud of glowing liquid to confuse their predators.

For each person on Earth...

there are 1,000 bristlemouth fish.

There are trillions of individual bristlemouth fish on the planet. That is far, *far* more than any other **vertebrates** – creatures with backbones.

Bristlemouths ●   Chickens ●   Humans ●   Rats ●

Each circle = 10 billion individuals

It's extremely difficult to count all the animals in the world accurately, so these are just scientists' best estimates.

confused Christopher Columbus.

On the 9th of January, 1493, while sailing across the Atlantic Ocean, Italian sailor Christopher Columbus saw three mermaids from his ship...

...they have a human appearance in the face, but are not half as beautiful as they are painted...*

*These are the actual words Columbus wrote in his log.

Columbus was actually seeing animals called **manatees**.

Scientists think that centuries of sailors' accounts of mermaids and mysterious women of the sea were probably manatees, seals and another type of sea mammal called a dugong.

Manatees are related to elephants, but they live in water. They are slow-moving plant-eaters that come to the surface to breathe.

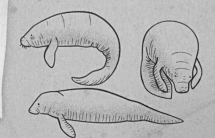

tell the history of an ocean.

Oceans are full of trillions of single-celled algae called **diatoms**. When diatoms die, they leave behind intricate, glass-like skeletons called **frustules**. These sink to the ocean floor and remain there forever...

Patch of sea floor, magnified 125x

Different diatoms are adapted to variations in temperatures, light and oxygen levels, and so on. This makes them different shapes and sizes. So scientists can read the history of a patch of ocean through the frustules left behind.

This species lived in warm water.

This species lived in cold water.

Scientists can find out how old each layer of the seabed is, so can work out when in Earth's history the ocean was hot, and when it was cold.

This frustule is from a freshwater species. At some point a river must have met the sea here.

This frustule is about 5 million years old, so this patch of ocean must have been here at least that long.

79 A Medieval assembly line...

turned Venice into a naval superpower.

Between the 13th and 16th centuries, Venice had the most powerful navy in the Mediterranean Sea. This was down to the city's fast and efficient ship-building industry, which used a system similar to an assembly line in a modern factory.

Construction began on land, where the ship's main body, or hull, was built.

1 Framing and planking

First, a light, sturdy frame was constructed in a dry dock. Then, planks were added to form the hull.

6 Components

Almost complete, the ships were fitted with ropes, anchors, sails and oars, all made in specialist workshops.

Ropes

Sails

Anchors

Oars

Food 7 Supplies

Kitchens prepared hard biscuits and salted meat and fish that would last through long voyages.

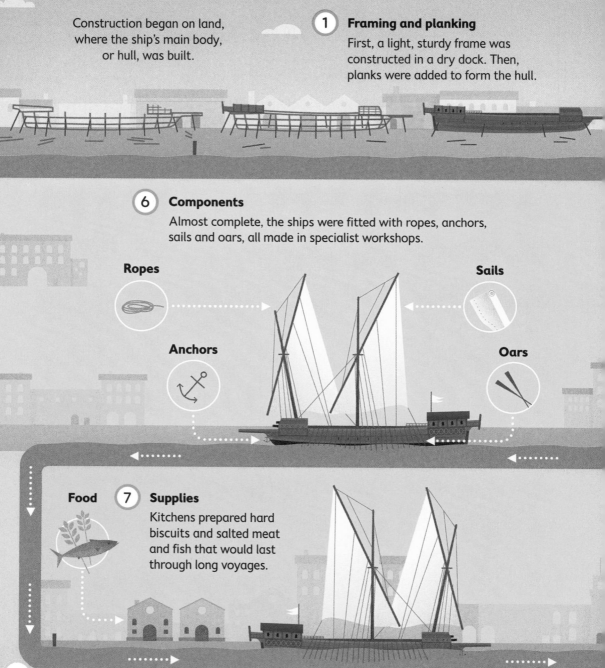

The area of Venice where ships were built was known as the **Arsenal**. At its peak, it employed 16,000 workers, each working in a specialized part of the process.

2 Caulking

To make the ship watertight, joins between planks were sealed with caulk – a mixture of hemp and sticky pitch made from pine resin.

3 Into the water

The hull was then lowered into a canal. From there, it was towed from one station or workshop to another for the next stages of construction and fitting.

5 Weapons

Next, the ships were loaded up with weapons. From the 16th century, merchant ships and warships were armed with heavy cannon.

Cannon

Cannonballs

Cannon carts

Gunpowder

4 Masts

Masts were pre-cut to standard lengths, ready to be fitted to the ships.

Pre-cut masts

Crew

8 Launch

By the end of the line, the ship was fully equipped and ready to set sail with a crew of at least 200 men.

80 Eels' eyes...

grow eight times bigger in the ocean.

When European and American eels are almost fully grown, they make their way from rivers to the Atlantic Ocean, to begin a journey of up to 10,000km (6,214 miles) to the Sargasso Sea, near Bermuda. Once in the ocean, their bodies undergo enormous changes.

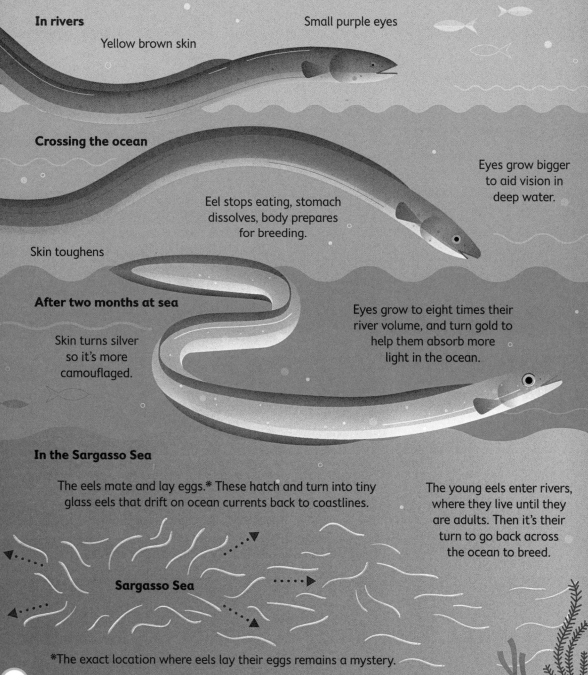

In rivers

Small purple eyes

Yellow brown skin

Crossing the ocean

Eyes grow bigger to aid vision in deep water.

Eel stops eating, stomach dissolves, body prepares for breeding.

Skin toughens

After two months at sea

Eyes grow to eight times their river volume, and turn gold to help them absorb more light in the ocean.

Skin turns silver so it's more camouflaged.

In the Sargasso Sea

The eels mate and lay eggs.* These hatch and turn into tiny glass eels that drift on ocean currents back to coastlines.

The young eels enter rivers, where they live until they are adults. Then it's their turn to go back across the ocean to breed.

Sargasso Sea

*The exact location where eels lay their eggs remains a mystery.

An upside-down world...
can be found beneath Antarctic ice.

99

Scientists have sent an underwater camera deep down beneath a massive shelf of ice in the Ross Sea, Antarctica. There, in the darkness, they discovered a remarkable upside-down world.

The camera beamed back photos of this topsy-turvy world to scientists waiting, the right way up, on the surface of the ice.

Upside-down creatures feed on the underside of the ice, just like other sea animals do on the sea floor.

Anemones burrow into the ice and hang upside-down.

Upside-down fish graze on algae.

Shrimp-like amphipods flit along upside-down.

82 Dead spacecraft...

rest in an undersea graveyard.

When a spacecraft breaks down or is no longer useful, it can be directed back to Earth. Much of it will burn up as it re-enters Earth's atmosphere, while the remaining pieces are crash-landed in the remotest part of the Pacific Ocean.

MIR
SPACE STATION

RUSSIAN
1986-2001

KOUNOTORI 4
CARGO CRAFT

JAPANESE
2013

This part of the ocean is the point on Earth furthest from any land – it's thousands of miles from anywhere.

Stuff crashing here doesn't pose an immediate threat to anybody – though the long-term effects of dumping all this space junk in the ocean are unknown.

PROGRESS 1-42
RESUPPLY SHIPS

RUSSIAN
1978-1990

ATV
TRANSFER VEHICLE

EUROPEAN
2008-2014

There are currently pieces of hundreds of spacecraft down there. One day in the coming years, the International Space Station will be sent down to join them.

83 The splash of a cannonball...

once marked a national border.

A country's national border doesn't exactly follow its coastline. In fact, its rights and powers may extend for miles beyond its shore. For several centuries, just *how* far was decided by the range of a cannon shot.

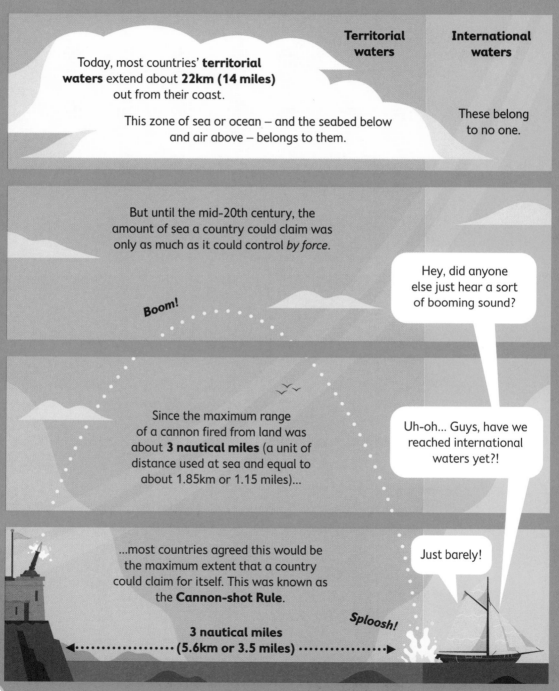

Territorial waters

International waters

Today, most countries' **territorial waters** extend about **22km (14 miles)** out from their coast.

This zone of sea or ocean – and the seabed below and air above – belongs to them.

These belong to no one.

But until the mid-20th century, the amount of sea a country could claim was only as much as it could control *by force*.

Boom!

Hey, did anyone else just hear a sort of booming sound?

Since the maximum range of a cannon fired from land was about **3 nautical miles** (a unit of distance used at sea and equal to about 1.85km or 1.15 miles)...

Uh-oh... Guys, have we reached international waters yet?!

...most countries agreed this would be the maximum extent that a country could claim for itself. This was known as the **Cannon-shot Rule**.

Just barely!

Sploosh!

3 nautical miles
←·················· (5.6km or 3.5 miles) ··················→

84 Lobsters caused a war...

between Brazil and France.

In the 1960s, a dispute broke out between Brazil and France over who was allowed to catch lobsters. The "Lobster War" ultimately boiled down to a single question: do lobsters walk or swim?

French fishers were chasing us here, in international waters off the coast of Brazil, where lots of us live on a ledge beneath the ocean.

Fishing laws held that boats from any country could catch creatures *swimming* in these waters...

...but only Brazilian boats were allowed to catch creatures that *walked* on the ledge.

In fact, we lobsters can do *both* — but wrangling between Brazil and France grew so heated that both countries sent warships to protect their fishing fleets.

After three years of simmering conflict, the law was changed, extending Brazilian territory to include the waters above the ledge. The warships sailed home.

85 Stowaway seeds...

once sailed around the world.

In old port cities, from New York to Antwerp, you can find plants from different regions around the world growing side by side. How did these plants all end up in one place? They were each, at one time, stowaways.

Love-in-a-mist
(from the Mediterranean region)

St. John's Wort
(from Europe)

Treacle-Mustard
(from northern
Europe and Asia)

**Love-lies-
bleeding**
(from the
American
tropics)

Before setting out, sailors loaded **ballast** – materials such as sand and gravel from local beaches – into their ships.

The ballast was arranged to balance a ship and its cargo, and make sure the vessel lay evenly in the water.

Ballast often contained plant seeds scooped up by accident. These were dumped on foreign shores when sailors had to make room for new cargo.

Some seeds sprouted and even flourished in their new homes, and could end up together in bouquets such as the one in this vase.

86 The best divers...

have the biggest spleens.

The Bajau people of Southeast Asia are famous divers. For a thousand years they have hunted fish on local reefs using little more than spears and goggles. Some Bajau divers can hold their breath underwater for up to 13 minutes. How? It may be down to a single organ: the spleen.

When we breathe, we take in oxygen, which is absorbed into red blood cells. The spleen can store some of those blood cells, releasing them when the body's oxygen levels are low.

The bigger the spleen, the more oxygen-rich red blood cells it can store. This means divers with bigger spleens will be able to hold their breath for longer.

The Bajau people have evolved spleens that are around

50% larger

than the average person's.

Average person's spleen

Bajau spleen

This allows them to dive more than 60m (200ft) on a single breath.

60% of a Bajau diver's working day can be spent under water, with no more equipment than spears, weights and goggles.

87 Maelstroms and doldrums...

can trap unwary sailors.

Out on the high seas, ships can encounter all sorts of extreme events
that can toss them overboard, or leave them stranded. Some are
predictable, but many can arise in an instant, with little warning...
In fact, a sea voyage can sometimes feel like a game of chance.

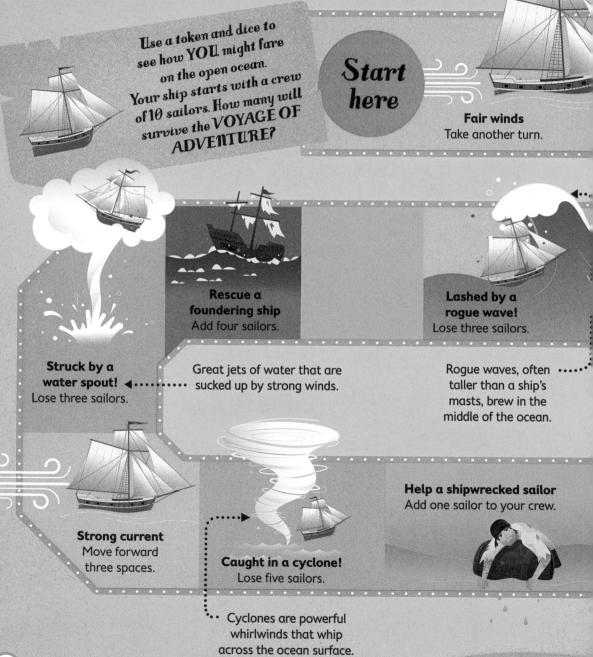

Use a token and dice to
see how YOU might fare
on the open ocean.
Your ship starts with a crew
of 10 sailors. How many will
survive the VOYAGE OF
ADVENTURE?

Start here

Fair winds
Take another turn.

Rescue a foundering ship
Add four sailors.

Lashed by a rogue wave!
Lose three sailors.

Struck by a water spout!
Lose three sailors.

Great jets of water that are
sucked up by strong winds.

Rogue waves, often
taller than a ship's
masts, brew in the
middle of the ocean.

Strong current
Move forward
three spaces.

Caught in a cyclone!
Lose five sailors.

Help a shipwrecked sailor
Add one sailor to your crew.

Cyclones are powerful
whirlwinds that whip
across the ocean surface.

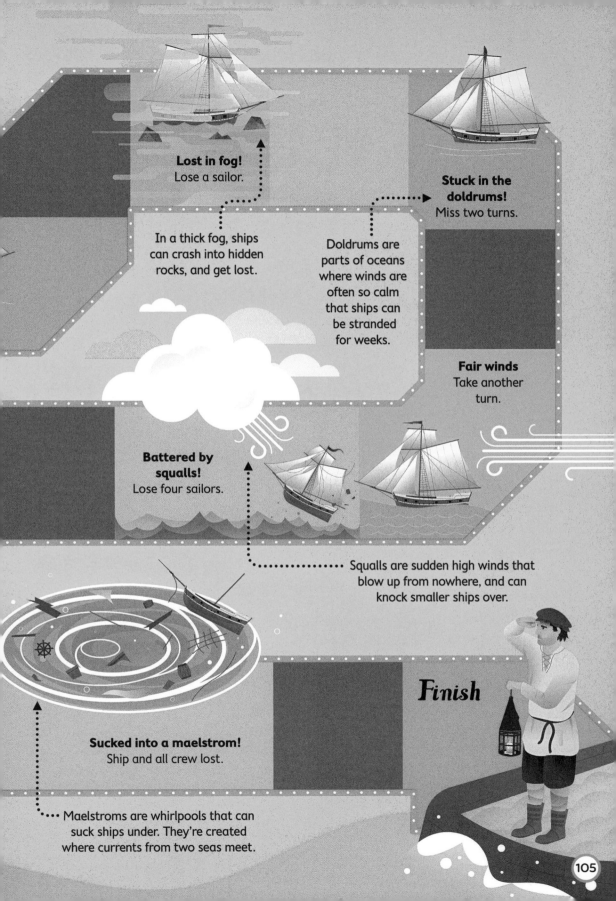

Lost in fog!
Lose a sailor.

In a thick fog, ships can crash into hidden rocks, and get lost.

Stuck in the doldrums!
Miss two turns.

Doldrums are parts of oceans where winds are often so calm that ships can be stranded for weeks.

Fair winds
Take another turn.

Battered by squalls!
Lose four sailors.

Squalls are sudden high winds that blow up from nowhere, and can knock smaller ships over.

Finish

Sucked into a maelstrom!
Ship and all crew lost.

Maelstroms are whirlpools that can suck ships under. They're created where currents from two seas meet.

may contain an unexpected ingredient.

OCEAN PLASTIC 2 THE REVENGE!

It is estimated that there are over 50 trillion pieces of microplastic in the ocean. Fish and shellfish swallow microplastic waste by mistake, and it can be absorbed into their bodies. These tiny pieces of plastic then make their way back to us in the fish and shellfish we eat.

"HUMANS FEED US THEIR PLASTIC...

...AND WE FEED IT RIGHT BACK TO THEM!"

Starring

TONS OF PLASTIC WASTE

featuring MICROBEADS IN MUSSELS! BOTTLE FRAGMENTS IN BREAM! PACKAGING IN POLLOCK!

"NOT TO BE IGNORED!" "WE MUST REDUCE PLASTIC WASTE!" "A MAJOR HEALTH HAZARD FOR ALL!"

89 Animals crossed the Pacific...

on floating debris.

In 2011, a massive wave, known as a **tsunami**, hit Japan, sweeping hundreds of animals out to sea. Several months later, many of these animals arrived back on dry land – but in North America.

Most of the creatures made the 6,500km (4,000 mile) trip on floating plastic junk, which can drift for years without rotting.

The animals included mussels, crabs, sea anemones, sea slugs, jellyfish, limpets, barnacles, worms and fish.

A floating dock carrying over 120 different types of animals landed in Oregon, USA, after

15 months
at sea.

After **2 years** at sea, a boat washed up on the coast of the of Washington State, USA, with six live fish inside.

In all, around 300 different species arrived in America – the largest number ever to travel so far at one time. Scientists are monitoring these incomers to see what effect their arrival might have on local wildlife.

90 Aquanauts and astronauts...

call an underwater science lab home.

Located off the coast of Key Largo in the Florida Keys, USA, **Aquarius Reef Base** sits 19m (62ft) below the surface. It is the only permanent underwater science lab in the world. Scientists stay there to study oceanic life, and astronauts prepare for life in space.

Run by Florida International University, the lab is used by scientists from all over the world.

The scientists – also called **aquanauts** – are able to live at the base for up to two weeks at a time.

By living in the base they are able to spend around 9 hours a day exploring the surrounding ocean.

The scientists study marine life and the effects of climate change and pollution on the ocean.

Over the years, a living skin of hard coral has grown up around the base, protecting it from damage.

NASA, the American space agency, uses the base for its NEEMO (NASA Extreme Environment Mission Operations) Program.

Astronauts on the NEEMO Program test new navigation techniques and technology for future space missions.

The undersea environment mimics the feeling of weightlessness in space. This allows astronauts to become used to using tools and working in bulky suits in low and zero gravity conditions.

The astronauts also test techniques for exploring the surface of the Moon, Mars and even asteroids.

We know that we *don't* know...

more than we *do* know about ocean wildlife.

In the early 2000s, hundreds of scientists from around the world started a 10-year mission to create the **World Register of Marine Species** (WoRMS for short) – a list of every named species in the oceans. They estimated that most of the ocean's creatures are still undiscovered.

KNOWN SPECIES

250,000

This number is changing all the time. Every year, around **2,000 new species** are discovered and named. And, every year, *some* known species come under threat.

THREATENED SPECIES

Some species are officially listed as **threatened** – meaning there aren't many individuals left in the wild, and they are in danger of dying out.

Total: unknown

There are currently well over **2,000** *known* threatened species, as well as lots that are *unknown*.

UNKNOWN SPECIES

Over 500,000

This is the number of species scientists *estimate* haven't yet been discovered and named.

Most of these species are likely to be shellfish, snails, slugs, crustaceans, zooplankton and phytoplankton, and it's likely that they're nearly all VERY tiny.

Every year, an unknown number of these unknown species becomes **threatened**.

EXTINCT SPECIES

Every year, an *unknown* number of known *and* unknown species become extinct, meaning they disappear from the oceans forever.

92 Even fish get seasick...

if you push them too hard.

Almost all people – and most land animals – will get sick when sailing across choppy waters. Seasickness makes animals dizzy and nauseous. Even fish aren't immune.

One scientist, who studies the brains of fish, found that he could make them helplessly dizzy by putting them in planes that simulate the weightlessness of outer space.

The planes climb steeply, then make a dive down from high altitude. This results in about 30 seconds of weightlessness inside the cabin.

According to the scientist, during the experiment several fish began to turn around in tight circles, and looked as if they were about to vomit.

93 Sailors can get land sick...

after long voyages.

The seasickness that many people experience in bad weather on ships is actually a kind of motion sickness that can be triggered in many different situations.

Motion sickness can strike...

...on a boat.

...on a camel.

...in a car.

Motion sickness is caused when the pattern of movement you *expect* doesn't match up with the movement you *feel*. This unsettles parts of the brain relating to balance, and causes a range of effects such as nausea, vomiting and cold sweats.

...in space.

...in virtual reality.

...on dry land.

Many sailors can adapt to the motion of a ship and overcome their seasickness. But, back on land, their brains don't instantly readjust. They often feel as though the ground is unsteady and moving beneath them. This "land sickness" can last for several days.

94 A ghost ship...
still haunts historians today.

In December 1872, sailors came across a ship, the *Mary Celeste*, rocking to and fro on choppy Atlantic waters. It was partly flooded, and its cargo was intact... but there was no one on board. It was a ghost ship.

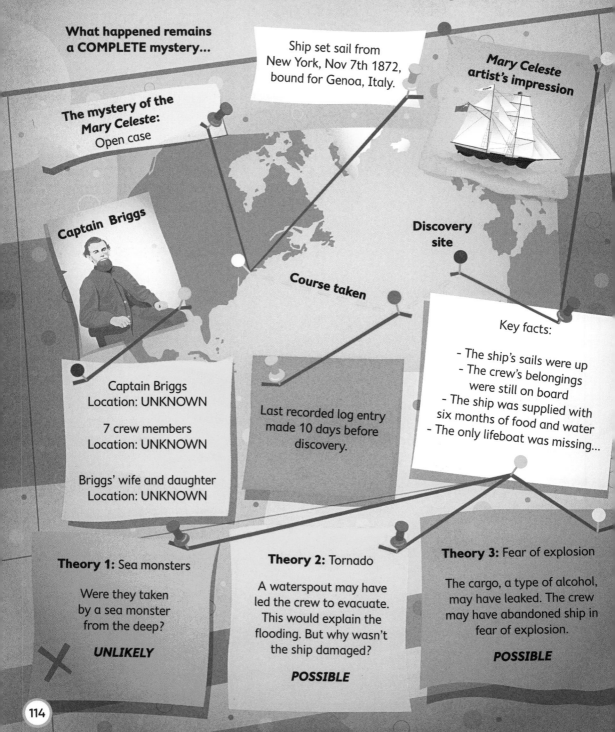

What happened remains a COMPLETE mystery...

Ship set sail from New York, Nov 7th 1872, bound for Genoa, Italy.

The mystery of the Mary Celeste: Open case

Mary Celeste artist's impression

Captain Briggs

Discovery site

Course taken

Captain Briggs
Location: UNKNOWN

7 crew members
Location: UNKNOWN

Briggs' wife and daughter
Location: UNKNOWN

Last recorded log entry made 10 days before discovery.

Key facts:

- The ship's sails were up
- The crew's belongings were still on board
- The ship was supplied with six months of food and water
- The only lifeboat was missing...

Theory 1: Sea monsters

Were they taken by a sea monster from the deep?

UNLIKELY

Theory 2: Tornado

A waterspout may have led the crew to evacuate. This would explain the flooding. But why wasn't the ship damaged?

POSSIBLE

Theory 3: Fear of explosion

The cargo, a type of alcohol, may have leaked. The crew may have abandoned ship in fear of explosion.

POSSIBLE

95 The crackle and pop...
of snapping shrimp could deafen you.

One common type of shrimp, known as a snapping shrimp, makes more noise than just about any other sea creature – all with the rapid snap of its powerful claws.

**Snapping shrimps' snaps
are so loud that...**

...hydrophones (underwater microphones) have recorded them at volumes of over **200 decibels**. That's as loud as a space rocket at take-off.

...the constant **CRACKLE** they make interferes with the communication systems on underwater drones and submarines.

...the shrimp use the **SNAP** to scare off predators and stun their prey, including crabs, worms and fish.

POP

CRACKLE

SNAP

POP

SNAP

CRACKLE

SNAP

POP

SNAP

The sound isn't actually made by one part of the shrimp's claw hitting the other. The rapid snapping action creates a bubble that collapses with a flash of light and a deafening **POP**.

SNAP

POP

POP

96 Unobtainable gold...

is scattered throughout the oceans.

For centuries, prospectors have mined gold from rocks under the ground, or sifted it from rocky riverbeds. But there's far, FAR more gold in the oceans. The trouble is, it's almost impossible to extract.

POP-POP

BZZ ZT

bLUBB
bLUBB

HISSSss

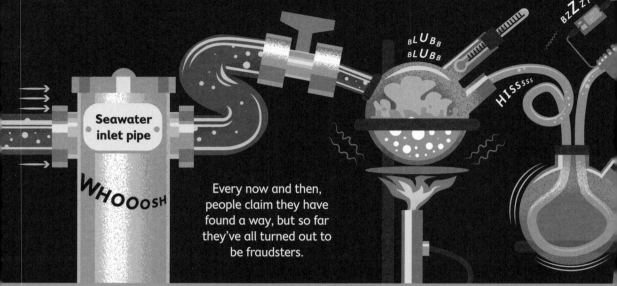

Seawater inlet pipe

WHOOOSH

Every now and then, people claim they have found a way, but so far they've all turned out to be fraudsters.

97 A submariner's bed...

is never empty.

On a submarine, every inch of space is precious, and there are often more sailors than beds. So, crew members share bunks and take turns to sleep.

A typical military submarine is about 100m (330ft) long, with a crew of around 100.

One third of the boat is taken up by its engines and steering. This leaves very little space for living and working.

This submarine is nuclear-powered. It doesn't need to refuel, and makes its own air and fresh water from seawater.

PLIP-PLIP-PLOOP-PLIP

SCHLOOP

SLOSH

Most of the gold in the oceans exists as dust particles smaller than grains of sand. To obtain

1 teaspoonful

of gold, you would need to evaporate *at least*

1 million tons

of seawater...

...and sift through all the bits of sand and salt left behind. But this process would cost far, FAR more than such a tiny amount of gold is worth.

Life on board often follows an 18-hour cycle: six hours of work, six hours of training and recreation, six hours of sleep.

When one submariner leaves the bunk to go on duty, another immediately rolls in. This is called **hot-bunking**.

Bunks may also be used to store extra supplies.

A submariner's bunk

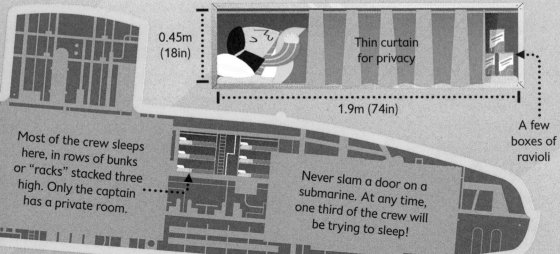

0.45m (18in)

Thin curtain for privacy

1.9m (74in)

A few boxes of ravioli

Most of the crew sleeps here, in rows of bunks or "racks" stacked three high. Only the captain has a private room.

Never slam a door on a submarine. At any time, one third of the crew will be trying to sleep!

98 It took 700 sheep...

to sail a Viking longship.

The Vikings were master boatbuilders whose ships were equally suited to shallow fjords or stormy seas. 1,000 years ago, they sailed around northern Europe, the Mediterranean and even across the Atlantic. But none of that would have been possible without sheep – *lots* of sheep.

Viking longships used large square sails made of wool from their flocks of sheep.

It took the wool of about **700 sheep** to make a single sail for a **30m (100ft)** longship.

20 boatbuilders could make a longship in about **six months**.

It might take **20 weavers** a **whole year** to make the sail.

99 The longest surfboard...

was reserved for royalty.

In ancient Hawaiian culture, all kinds of people surfed: women and men, rich and poor. Three hundred years ago, anyone could surf on an *alaia* (ah-LIE-ah) – but only a chosen few could ride an *olo* (OH-low)...

An olo was a kind of surfboard about
6m (20 feet)
long.

Only kings, queens and priests were allowed to use these special surfboards.

They were best suited to long rides on low, sloping waves.

Commoners usually surfed on alaias – boards about
3m (10 feet)
long.

Alaias were best suited to shorter rides on steep, fast, breaking waves.

Today, longer, more stable surfboards tend to be used by beginners, while expert surfers use shorter boards to perform difficult tricks.

100 Seafaring tigers...

can swim across the open sea.

Although many cats avoid water, tigers are strong swimmers. They can actually swim for many miles across deep water, and may actively chase animals into water to catch them more easily.

Tigers have been known to swim distances of **15km (9 miles)** in the sea, and can go twice as far in rivers.

Sumatran tigers – a type of tiger living in Indonesia – even have webbed toes, making them excellent long-distance swimmers.

Sumatran tigers are known to cross from island to island in search of new territory and prey.

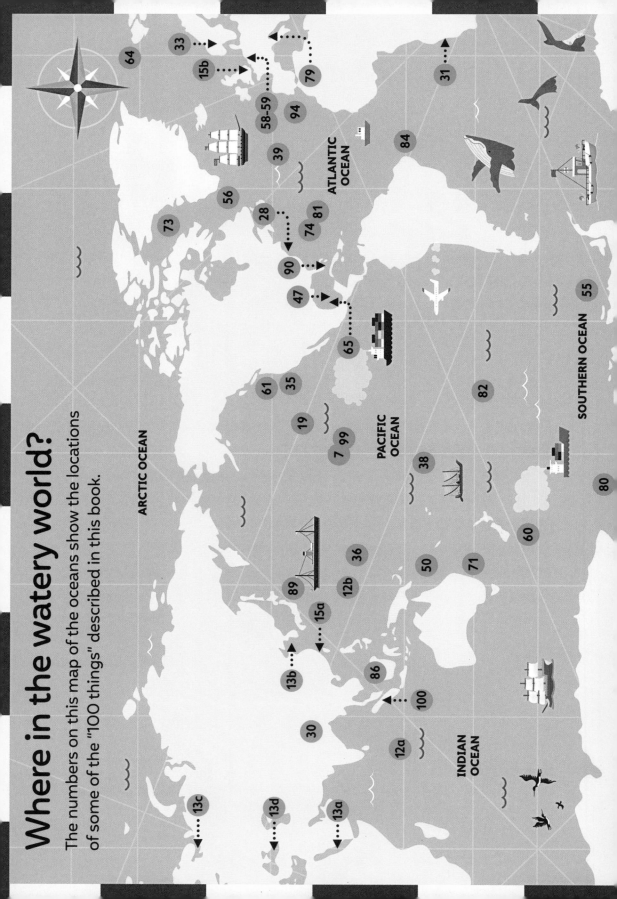

Where in the watery world?

The numbers on this map of the oceans show the locations of some of the "100 things" described in this book.

ARCTIC OCEAN

ATLANTIC OCEAN

PACIFIC OCEAN

INDIAN OCEAN

SOUTHERN OCEAN

7 Black sand beaches in Hawai'i

12a Ancient glass sponges can be found here

12b The Mariana Trench, the deepest ocean trench

13a The Red Sea

13b The Yellow Sea

13c The White Sea

13d The Black Sea

15a Start of the Great Tea Race in Fuzhou

15b Finish of the Great Tea Race in London

19 The Great Pacific Garbage Patch

28 The site where Alvin sank – and was rescued ten months later

30 Mount Everest – once part of the ocean floor

31 The Skeleton Coast

33 Scandinavia, where the ocean has 200 names

35 Kelp forests can be found along this coast

36 Bikini Atoll

38 Polynesia – a vast region scattered with tiny islands

39 The mid-Atlantic mountain range

47 The Hot Tub of Despair

50 This is where Sandy Island should be – but isn't

55 Likely source of the Bloop

56 Greenland sharks grow up here

58-59 The Netherlands

60 Subantarctic Islands

61 Godzilla, Mothra, Sasquatch

64 The place where Fram emerged from the ice

65 Migrating woodpeckers

71 Octopolis

73 Good kayaks built here

74 The Sargasso Sea

79 The city of Venice

80 This is where eels lay their eggs

81 The Ross Sea and its upside-down world

82 Spacecraft cemetery

84 The Lobster War took place here

86 The Bajau people live and dive in this region

89 Tsunami strikes Japan in 2011

90 Aquarius Reef Base

94 Mary Celeste discovered

99 Olos and alaias used here

100 Swimming tigers in Sumatra

Glossary

This glossary explains some of the words used in this book.
Words written in *italic* type have their own entries.

algae A plant-like type of organism, including seaweed, that generally grows in or near water

aquanauts Underwater explorers

atmosphere The layer of gases surrounding the Earth

bacteria Microscopic living things, found all over the world

ballast Heavy material such as sand or gravel put in the bottom of a ship to keep it stable

bioluminescence The ability of certain living things to make their own light

black smokers A type of *hydrothermal vent* that spews out black clouds

bow The front part of a boat's *hull*

brine Very salty water

camouflage Shading or patterns that help to hide something in its surroundings

carbon dioxide A gas that causes the atmosphere to trap heat

cargo Things carried from one place to another, usually on a ship

castaway Someone who has been shipwrecked and stranded

chromatophores Specialized cells inside creatures such as cuttlefish, that control their *camouflage*

clipper A type of speedy sailing ship

container A large metal box used to transport *cargo* around the world

coral A type of *invertebrate* that lives in shallow waters and forms *reefs*

cores Samples drilled out of the *seabed* to study

current A continuous flow of water in one direction through a sea or ocean

dead zone An area of ocean with little or no oxygen, often due to *pollution*

deck The flat surface between the sides of a ship's *hull*, where sailors stand and work

dehydration When somebody loses more water than they take in and become very ill

diatoms Tiny, single-celled *algae* that live in the ocean

dinoflagellates Aquatic *phytoplankton* that are often *bioluminescent*

doldrums Patches of still ocean with very little wind, where sailing ships can get stuck

fossil The shape or remains of a dead plant or animal, preserved in rock

freighter A large ship designed to carry heavy or bulky *cargo*, often in *containers*

ghost nets Fishing nets lost or thrown away at sea, which continue to catch fish

gyre A huge swirling set of *currents*, creating a large circle

hull The main body and framework of a boat

hydrophone A microphone designed for listening to sounds underwater

hydrothermal vent A crack in the sea bed near a volcano, that shoots out hot water

iceberg A large piece of ice that has broken off a glacier or ice shelf and floated out to sea

international waters Patches of sea or ocean that do not belong to, and are not governed by the laws of, any particular country

invertebrate A type of animal without a backbone

kayak A lightweight covered boat, usually for one person, with a paddle

keel The hard structure along the bottom of a boat that keeps it stable

lava Hot, molten rock which flows from volcanoes

lifeboat A small boat kept on a larger ship to escape in an emergency

longship A long, narrow ship powered by sails or by rowing, used by ancient Vikings

manatee A type of mammal that lives in the ocean, sometimes known as a sea cow

mangrove A type of tree that can grow in saltwater, and has long roots like stilts

mast An upright post on a boat that holds the *sails*

masthead The highest part of a boat's *mast*

microplastics Tiny pieces of plastic smaller than 5mm (0.2 inches)

migration Mass movement of creatures from one place to another

nautical mile A unit used to measure distances at sea, equivalent to 1.85km (1.15 miles)

photosynthesis The way green plants convert sunlight into energy

phytoplankton Microscopic plant-like living things that drift through the ocean. Some are plants, some are *bacteria*

pollution Substances such as waste and chemicals that are introduced into the environment and cause damage

propeller A mechanical device that spins underwater to move a boat forward

reef A mass of *coral* or rocks in shallow water. Home to a huge variety of *species*.

sail A piece of material attached to a *mast* that can catch the wind and propel a boat through the sea

seabed The bottom of the ocean

sea level The average height of the sea's surface where it meets land

shanty A song traditionally sung by sailors on boats to help them as they work

shoal A huge number of fish swimming together. If the fish in the group are all swimming in the same direction and at the same speed, it is described as a school.

species A particular type of plant, animal or other living thing

stern The back part of a boat's *hull*

submarine An underwater vehicle that can make long journeys independently

submersible A small vehicle designed to explore under the sea, which usually relies on a support vessel at the surface

symbiosis When creatures from two different *species* have a relationship that helps both of them

tectonic plates Large pieces of land that make up the Earth's crust

territorial waters The area of sea extending from a shore that belongs to that country. This is generally up to 14 miles (22km), where it becomes *international waters*.

trash vortex A swirling mass of waste and *microplastics*, in the middle of a *gyre*

tsunami A huge wave, often triggered by an earthquake beneath the *seabed*

venom Poison that an animal injects into prey or an attacker

vertebrate A type of animal with a backbone

zooplankton Microscopic animal-like living things that drift through the ocean

ANATOMY OF A SAILING SHIP: THE TEA CLIPPER

Masthead

Mast

Sail

Deck

Stern

Bow

Hull

Keel

Index

To get this book afloat...
a whole crew had to haul away together.

Research and writing by
Jerome Martin, Alex Frith, Alice James,
Lan Cook, Minna Lacey and Lizzie Cope

Layout and design by
Jenny Offley, Winsome D'Abreu, Tilly Kitching,
Lenka Hrehova and Samuel Gorham

Illustration by
Dominique Byron, Dale Edwin Murray,
Federico Mariani, Shaw Nielsen and Jake Williams

With expert advice from
Dr. Roger Trend and
Dr. Jack H. Laverick

Series editor: Ruth Brocklehurst
Series designer: Stephen Moncrieff

We bound this book with tar and twine
Haul away, haul away
A mermaid's comb runs through its spine
Now haul away, me hearties!

First published in 2021 by Usborne Publishing Ltd., Usborne House, 83-85 Saffron Hill, London, EC1N 8RT, United Kingdom, usborne.com Copyright © 2021 Usborne Publishing Ltd. The name Usborne and the Balloon logo are trade marks of Usborne Publishing Ltd. All rights reserved. No part of this publication may be reproduced, stored in any retrieval system, or transmitted in any form or by any means, electronic, mechanical, photocopying, recording or otherwise, without the prior permission of Usborne Publishing Ltd. First published in America 2021, UE, EDC, Tulsa, Oklahoma 74146 usbornebooksandmore.com Library of Congress Control Number: 2020915806